Homilies from the Heart
YEAR B

Msgr. Robert D. Fuller

Published by
KAN Distributing Inc.

Copyright 2010, Msgr. Robert D. Fuller

All rights reserved. No part of this publication may be reproduced, stored in a retrieval system, or transmitted in any form or by any means—electronic, mechanical, photocopy, recording, or any other—except for brief quotations in printed reviews, without the prior permission of the publisher.

Biblical citation abbreviations are consistent with The Chicago Manual of Style, 14th Edition, 1993.

The Book Team:
Ernie Nedder, Publisher
Kathy Nedder, CFO
Msgr. Robert D. Fuller, Author
Sharon Nicks of Types, Graphic Design

Printed in the United States
KAN Distributing

Individual Copies: $12.00

Ordering Information
Check local bookstores
From the author: 520-326-7670
or email: cabrini1962@aol.com
Order #KAN1606

ISBN: 978-0-9841716-2-0

DEDICATION

This book is dedicated in gratitude to God for the wonderful vocation of priesthood, to my family, to Adolfo Quezada and Katherine Smith, who made this book possible, and to all the loving people who have encouraged me through the years.

Msgr. Robert D. Fuller

Any profit from this book will be donated to the Catholic Worker House, Casa Maria, in Tucson, Arizona

TABLE OF CONTENTS

Foreword xi

Preface 1

FIRST SUNDAY OF ADVENT
(Is 63:16b-17, 19b; 64:2-7; 1 Cor 1:3-9; Mk 13:33-37) 3

SECOND SUNDAY OF ADVENT
(Is 40:1-5, 9-11; 2 Pt 3:8-14; Mk 1:1-8) 7

THIRD SUNDAY OF ADVENT
(Is 61:1-2, 10-11; 1 Thes 5:16-24; Jn 1:6-8, 19-28) 10

FOURTH SUNDAY OF ADVENT
(2 Sm 7:1-5, 8b-12, 14a-16; Rom 16:25-27; Lk 1:26-38) 13

CHRISTMAS
(Is 9:1-6; Ti 2:11-14; Lk 2:1-14) 16

HOLY FAMILY
(Gn 15:1-6; 21:1-3; Heb 11:8; 11-12, 17-19; Lk 2:22, 39-40) .. 20

EPIPHANY
(Is 60:1-6; Eph 3:2-3a, 5-6; Mt 2:1-12) 24

BAPTISM OF JESUS
(Is 55:1-11; 1Jn 5:1-9; Mk 1:7-11) 27

SECOND SUNDAY OF THE YEAR
(1 Sam 3:3b-10, 19; 1 Cor 6:13c-15a, 17-20; Jn 1:35-42) 30

THIRD SUNDAY OF THE YEAR
(Jon 3:1-5, 10; 1 Cor 7:29-31; Mk 1:14-20) 33

FOURTH SUNDAY OF THE YEAR
(Dt 18:15-20; 1 Cor 7:32-35; Mk 1:21-28) 36

FIFTH SUNDAY OF THE YEAR
(Jb 7:1-4, 6-7; 1 Cor 9:16-19, 22-23; Mk 1:29-39) 40

SIXTH SUNDAY OF THE YEAR
(Lv 13:1-2, 44-46; 1 Cor 10:31, 11:1; Mk 1:40-45) 43

SEVENTH SUNDAY OF THE YEAR
(Is 43:18-19, 21-22, 24b-25; 2 Cor 1:18-22; Mk 2:1-12) 46

EIGHTH SUNDAY OF THE YEAR
(Hos 2:16b, 17b, 21-22; 2 Cor 3:1-6; Mk 2:18-22) 51

FIRST SUNDAY OF LENT
(Gn 9:8-15; 1 Pt 3:18-22; Mk 1:12-15) 52

SECOND SUNDAY OF LENT
(Gn 22:1-2, 9a, 10-13, 15-18; Rom 8:31b-34; Mk 9:2-10) .. 55

THIRD SUNDAY OF LENT
(Ex 20:1-17; 1 Cor 1:22-25; Jn 2:13-25) 59

FOURTH SUNDAY OF LENT
(2 Chr 36:14-16, 19-23; Eph 2:4-10; Jn 3:14-21) 62

FIFTH SUNDAY OF LENT
(Jer 31:31-34; Heb 5:7-9; Jn 12:20-33) 65

PALM SUNDAY
.... 68

EASTER SUNDAY
(Acts 10:34a, 37-43; Col 3:1-4; Jn 20:1-9) 70

SECOND SUNDAY OF EASTER
(Acts 4:32-35; 1 Jn 5:1-6; Jn 20:19-31) 73

THIRD SUNDAY OF EASTER
(Acts 3:13-15, 17-19; 1 Jn 2:1-5a; Lk 24:35-48) 76

FOURTH SUNDAY OF EASTER
(Acts 4:8-12; 1 Jn 3:1-2; Jn 10:11-18) 79

FIFTH SUNDAY OF EASTER
(Acts 9:26-31; 1 Jn 3:18-24; Jn 15:1-8) 83

SIXTH SUNDAY OF EASTER
(Acts 10:25-26, 34-35, 44-48; 1 Jn 4:7-10; Jn 15:9-17) 86

SEVENTH SUNDAY OF EASTER
(Acts 1:15-17, 20a, 20c-26; 1 Jn 4:11-16; Jn 17:11b-19) 89

PENTECOST
(Acts 2:1-11; 1 Cor 12:3b-7, 12-13; Jn 20:19-23) 93

TRINITY SUNDAY
(Dt 4:32-34; Rom 8:14-17; Mt 28:16-20) 96

BODY AND BLOOD OF CHRIST
(Ex 24:3-8; Heb 9:11-15; Mk 14:12-16, 22-26) 99

BIRTH OF JOHN THE BAPTIST
(Is 49:1-6; Acts 13:22-26; Lk 1:57-66, 80) 102

FEAST OF SAINTS PETER AND PAUL
(Acts 12:1-11; 2 Tm 4:6-8, 17-18; Mt 16:13-19) 106

TWELFTH SUNDAY OF THE YEAR
(Job 38:1, 8-11; 2 Cor 5:14-17; Mk 4:35-41) 110

THIRTEENTH SUNDAY OF THE YEAR
(Wis 1:13-15, 2:23-24; 2 Cor 8:7-9, 13-15;
Mk 5:21-24, 35b-43) 113

FOURTEENTH SUNDAY OF THE YEAR
(Ez 2:2-5; 2 Cor 12:7-10; Mk 6:1-6) 116

FIFTEENTH SUNDAY OF THE YEAR
(Am 7:12-15; Eph 1:3-14; Mk 6:7-13) 120

SIXTEENTH SUNDAY OF THE YEAR
(Jer 23:1-6; Eph 2:13-16; Mk 6:30-34) 123

SEVENTEENTH SUNDAY OF THE YEAR
(2 Kgs 4:42-44; Eph 4:1-6; Jn 6:1-15) 127

EIGHTEENTH SUNDAY OF THE YEAR
(Ex 16:2-4, 12-15; Eph 4:17, 20-24; Jn 6:24-35) 130

NINETEENTH SUNDAY OF THE YEAR
(1 Kgs 19:4-8; Eph 4:30, 5:2; Jn 6:41-51) 133

TWENTIETH SUNDAY OF THE YEAR
(Prv 9:1-6; Eph 5:15-20; Jn 6:51-58) 136

TWENTY-FIRST SUNDAY OF THE YEAR
(Josh 24:1-2a, 15-17, 18b; Eph 5:21-32; Jn 6:60-69) 139

TWENTY-SECOND SUNDAY OF THE YEAR
(Dt 4:1-2, 6-8; Jas 1:17-18, 21b-22, 27;
Mk 7:1-8, 14-15, 21-23) 142

TWENTY-THIRD SUNDAY OF THE YEAR
(Is 35:4-7a; Jas 2:1-5; Mk 7:31-37) 145

TRIUMPH OF THE CROSS
(Num 21:4b-9; Phil 2:6-11; Jn 3:13-17) 148

TWENTY-FOURTH SUNDAY OF THE YEAR
(Is 50:5-9a; Jas 7:14-18; Mk 8:27-35) 151

TWENTY-FIFTH SUNDAY OF THE YEAR
(Wis 2:12, 17-20; Jas 3:16, 4:3; Mk 9:30-37) 154

Twenty-Sixth Sunday of the Year
(Nm 11:25-29; Jas 5:1-6; Mk 9:38-43, 45, 47-48) 157

Twenty-Seventh Sunday of the Year
(Gn 2:18-24; Heb 2:9-11; Mk 10:2-16) 160

Twenty-Eighth Sunday of the Year
(Wis 7:7-11; Heb 4:12-13; Mk 10:17-30) 164

Twenty-Ninth Sunday of the Year
(Is 53:10-11; Heb 4:14-16; Mk 10:35-45) 167

Thirtieth Sunday of the Year
(Jer 31:7-9; Heb 5:1-6; Mk 10:46-52) 170

Thirty-First Sunday of the Year
(Dt 6:2-6; Heb 7:23-28; Mk 12:28b-34) 173

Thirty-Second Sunday of the Year
(Kg 17:10-16; Heb 9:24-28; Mk 12:38-44) 176

Thirty-Third Sunday of the Year
(Dn 12:1-3; Heb 10:11-14, 18; Mk 13:24-32) 179

Christ the King
(Dn 7:13-19; Rv 1:5-8; Jn 18:33b-37) 182

FOREWORD

In a culture and society filled with mass media and advanced methods of communicating you might think that preaching is outdated, passé, no longer relevant. But when you talk to people in a parish community, where a priest preaches well every Sunday, you realize preaching remains important. God's word preached with passion and conviction still matters, still touches people in significant ways by moving hearts and even transforming lives.

Monsignor Robert D. Fuller, a priest of the Diocese of Tucson, is such a preacher.

Always prepared, he breaks open God's Word in a way that stirs hearts and deepens hunger for the Lord. Monsignor Fuller speaks in concrete language, uses human experience, and always remains faithful to the scriptural text. He makes a bishop proud.

Many research studies have revealed the hunger people have for good preaching. They want homilies that are spiritual, thoughtful, meaningful, and that move them into a closer relationship with God. *Homilies from the Heart* contains such homilies. Over the liturgical year, Monsignor Fuller uses a variety of ways to lead people into deeper contact with the scriptures.

The people of St. Frances Cabrini Parish brag about his homilies, delight in them, and are fed by them. As you read *Homilies from the Heart,* you will see why his people consider themselves blessed.

These homilies will provide preachers with much food for thought and will provide homiletic teachers with good examples of what preaching can and should be. The spiritual messages found in this book will inspire you and stay with you!

Most Reverend Gerald F. Kicanas, D.D.
Bishop of Tucson

PREFACE

The publication of my first book, *Homilies from the Heart*, Year A of the lectionary cycle, was a leap of faith. I had no idea how it would be received or how many people would purchase it. I was cautioned that the power of homilies is listening to them, not reading them. Obviously, the publication of volumes two and three, years B and C depended upon a positive response.

The response to book A has been both exciting and humbling to me. I am excited that so many people want it. I am excited by comments of how helpful it has been on their spiritual journey. I am humbled that God would use me as an instrument to provide this help. I am humbled because I know that I am nothing nor have nothing that has not been given to me.

I am especially grateful to Adolfo Quezada, an author of several books on spiritual life. Adolfo convinced me to publish these homilies and has worked tirelessly to bring them to reality. I am also grateful to Ernie and Kathy Nedder and their KAN Distributing, Inc., for publishing what I judge to be very attractive books.

The Casa Maria soup kitchen in South Tucson has received substantial help from the first book. They will continue to be the recipient of any profits from the second book.

I am happy to present *Homilies from the Heart,* year B, based on the Gospel of Mark, and pray that it will bring you in some way closer to our loving God.

Msgr. Robert D. Fuller
June 11, 2010

📖 The First Sunday of Advent
(Is 63:16b-17, 19b; 64:2-7; 1 Cor 1:3-9; Mk 13:33-37)

Recently, in the comic strip, "For Better or Worse," Dad is intently reading a document when his six-year-old son Michael comes in and asks, "Whatcha reading Daddy?" "A life insurance policy," Dad replies. "What's that Daddy?" "Well," Dad explains, "if I died, life insurance would cover the cost of the funeral and lots of other expenses too." "Oh," says Michael, a little scared at the thought of his Daddy dying. "It's a difficult subject to discuss," Dad says, "We have no idea when that may happen, but it's good to be prepared because when it happens money is very important to have." Michael then asks a question Dad didn't expect, "Dad, how much are you worth?"

This story ushers us into a new Church year with the season of Advent. It reminds us of how precious our life is, how limited our time is, and how much we are worth to Jesus. Our Gospel is about watchful, prayerful waiting for the coming of the Lord. Actually, Advent is really about the two comings of the Lord.

Jesus' first coming was at Christmas. In a few weeks we will be totally involved with the beautiful Christmas story. Do we find Christmas scary? No way! It's all about love, peace, and salvation. But we begin Advent today with a Gospel about Jesus' second coming.

Jesus said, "Be watchful, be alert. You do not know when the Lord is coming. May he not come and find you sleeping. So I say to all, watch." Do we find this gospel scary? I hope not. Jesus did not say, "Be afraid." He tells us to be watchful and alert, which is very different from running scared. Advent is about watchful waiting. There are different kinds of waiting. We wait for an event and we know exactly when it will happen. That's like Christmas. We wait for an event and we have no idea when it will happen. That's the second coming of Jesus at the end of the world, or to put it in more meaningful terms, the coming of Jesus for us whenever our time comes.

St. Augustine wrote that it is by design that Jesus hid the last day from us so that we would be on the lookout for him every day of our lives. That's a wonderful design, that we do not know our own future. Practically speaking, this means that we will live now as we want to live then. We will live our precious lives and use our precious time in the expectation of the Lord's coming for us.

Oh, but this human nature of ours. It's hard to get too excited unless we are faced with something more certain, more imminent. But nothing could be more certain than the fact that we have limited time, and the fact that the Lord is coming for us someday. But someday just does not seem real enough for us, so we find ourselves saying things like, "I'll break this habit when things settle down." Or, "I'll pray more when I get older." Or, "I'll be more generous when I have enough money." Or, "I know I can be more loving and I will be one of these days." All of this means that we tend to live our lives as though this is a dress rehearsal rather than the real thing. That's why we have Advent. Be watchful, be alert. Don't be found sleeping when the Lord comes. In other words, we are living now our one and only real life.

Imagine how fully we will live if this Advent message gets through to us. Imagine one day of watchful and alert living. To whom would we say again, "I love you"? How would we show our love? From whom would we ask forgiveness? Would not our whole day be filled with acts of kindness and love? There would be no room for anger or revenge. We would have no time for quarreling, holding grudges, or refusing to forgive. We simply would have no time for anything that was not about loving. Just imagine that.

Thank you, Lord, for Advent. Thank you for calling us to be, not fearful, but watchful and alert. Thank you, Lord, because when Advent really touches our hearts we will know the love, the peace, and the joy that Christmas – and every day – is about.

📖 The Second Sunday of Advent
(Is 40:1-5, 9-11; 2 Pt 3:8-14; Mk 1:1-8)

It is now the Second Sunday of Advent. Last week we said Advent is a time of watchful waiting, expectation, and anticipation for Christ's coming at Christmas and his coming at the end of time. Last week we began Advent with a gospel about watchful waiting for Jesus' Second Coming. Today, we back up to the beginning of Mark's Gospel which is about Jesus' first coming.

Someone said that every person needs something to look forward to in life in order to survive. Advent gives us plenty to look forward to.

Today we see John the Baptist, the powerful voice of one crying out in the desert, "Prepare the way of the Lord, make straight his paths." Picture this powerful man, tall, rawboned, dressed in camel's hair, with a leather belt around his waist. He fed on locusts and wild honey. And what did he proclaim? "One mightier than I is coming after me. I am not worthy to stoop and loosen the thongs of his sandals."

What are you saying, John? You are the mightiest prophet of

your day. You are not worthy to untie his shoes? Who could this mightier one be? I remember a church sign in December which read, "Someone is coming." Who is this someone? We know who he is. He is as mighty as God because he is God become man. We celebrate his arrival in a few days. Isn't he worth an Advent of watchful waiting? Isn't his arrival something to look forward to?

As remarkable as Christmas is, as unbelievable as Christmas is, the truth of Christmas can easily get lost in the frenzy of the days ahead. Advent calls us to stillness. But it is difficult for us to be still. We get caught in the pressures that make Advent the most frantic time of the year.

St. Francis de Sales wrote that, "True waiting means waiting without anxiety." Advent is the time for walking slowly when others are rushing. It is a time for traveling lightly when consumers are burdened with merchandise. Advent is a time for eating less when others are eating more, and for focusing inward when others go from party to party.

Let's focus inward for a minute. Let's get in touch with this remarkable, unbelievable truth of Christmas. Let's imagine that Christmas never happened. Let's imagine this mighty one did not arrive. How different would our world be? How different would we be? This would not be the year 2010; it would be the Jewish year 5,771. There would be no Jesus of

Nazareth. We would not know the meaning of the words, "a savior is born." We would live with our sins. We would not be here today because there would be no Church, Mass, or Eucharist. God would be distant and frightening because no one would have assured us that God is our loving Father. We would die without the hope of eternal life. Just imagine if Christmas had never happened. But it did. If everyone needs something to look forward to in life in order to survive, see what we have to look forward to.

Bishop Fulton Sheen wrote that, "These human hearts of ours can be hard enough, heaven knows. They can hold out in cold, stubborn pride against many a tender plea and gentle overture. Still, the human heart must have a melting point. The melting point must be the cave, and the manger, and God crying – a baby."

This is who we are waiting for. This is what Advent is all about. Let's not miss it. Let's savor it in the days to come.

The Third Sunday of Advent
(Is 61:1-2, 10-11; 1 Thes 5:16-24; Jn 1:6-8, 19-28)

'Tis the season to be jolly. I wish you a Merry Christmas. Joy to the world. Do you feel like saying, "Stop it! If I hear jolly, merry, or joy one more time, I will scream"? Does it seem like everyone is expected to put on a smiley face this time of year? If we don't, people may call us a scrooge. People may say, "What's wrong with you? Get with it." Nobody wants to be a scrooge, so we paint over the harsh reality of our lives with a happy face. Do you ever feel this way?

Now, to make things even worse, this Third Sunday of Advent is called Rejoice Sunday. Isaiah says, "I rejoice heartily in the Lord." The psalm says, "My soul rejoices in my God." And Paul tells us to "Rejoice always." What is our Church doing? Is our Church playing some kind of cruel trick on us? Come on, life is not that way. Come on, we know better than that. When we meet people we ask, "How are you?" Most times that is just a polite question. We hope they won't tell us how they really are because most likely it will be another tale of woe. Come on now, that's reality.

So is Rejoice Sunday pollyannaish or unrealistic? Is it some kind of game? Hardly! The calls to rejoice that came from God's word today are not divorced from reality. In fact, they come from reality harsher than we will ever live.

Isaiah said, "I rejoice heartily in the Lord." Who was Isaiah? He was a prophet when everything was going wrong and people would not listen to anything he said. But because he kept speaking out, he was about to be killed when he wrote, "I rejoice heartily in the Lord." Paul said, "Rejoice always." Was Paul speaking from a life that was a bowlful of cherries? Paul experienced beatings, shipwreck, imprisonment, and finally was beheaded. And he wrote, "Rejoice, always."

And then there's Jesus. Was life fair to Jesus? Right before he was betrayed he said, "All this I tell you that my joy may be yours and your joy may be complete." These calls to rejoice are not divorced from reality. They come from reality harsher than we shall know.

So what does all of this mean? We have our struggles in life. We may be struggling with a tense and difficult marriage or family relationship. We may be struggling to make ends meet. We may be struggling with health problems. And Isaiah, Paul, and Jesus are not asking us to deny or cover up our pain. God wants us to be joyful in spite of our problems. Is this possible? Yes! God's word today is calling us to get underneath our struggle and pain. It is calling us to the deepest part of our being where we can find faith and trust. This faith and trust is not make-believe. It is so real that it makes the difference between life with a purpose and complete cynicism.

So what does God want us to trust and believe in? He wants us to believe in his love for us. He wants us to trust that love, no matter how distant it seems sometimes. God wants us to believe that we are bigger than we think, and that our lives are bigger and more important than they seem. He wants us to believe that we are part of a living reality that is much bigger than our struggle and pain. God wants us to trust that he knows what he is doing and that he does everything in love, a love so real that he sent his only son to be one of us. He sent a baby born at Christmas, a baby who would grow up in the unfairness of life and who would say to us, "I want my joy to be yours. I want your joy to be complete."

Believe and trust in that love, my friends, and it will be.

The Fourth Sunday of Advent
(2 Sm 7:1-5, 8b-12, 14a-16; Rom 16:25-27; Lk 1:26-38)

Last week we reflected on how God calls us to faith and trust, a faith and trust so real that we will be joyful people in spite of our struggles and pain. It is now the last Sunday of Advent. For weeks we have been waiting, expecting the arrival of the Mighty One. Today it is coming very near. It is about to happen because of the faith and trust of a 15-year-old maiden named Mary.

After last week's call to believe and trust, today God is showing us what he means. Today's gospel gives us a model of trusting who is truly remarkable. Sure, today's gospel is familiar to us, perhaps so familiar that we miss its full impact. So let's get into the reality of what is happening in our gospel.

Today Luke announces the conception of this Mighty One. Picture Mary, a 15-year-old girl betrothed to Joseph. Now the most startling and strange moment of her life happens. In scripture angels are messengers. It does not mean that Mary actually saw an angel, but she certainly did get a message. "Hail, full of grace, the Lord is with you." What a greeting to such a young one. As we would expect, Mary was greatly troubled at what was said and pondered what sort of greeting this might be. In our language, Mary wondered, "What's going on here?"

"Do not be afraid, Mary, for you have found favor with God." "Oh sure, that's easy to say, 'Do not be afraid,' but what do you mean, 'You have found favor with God'? What is this all about?" "Behold, you will conceive in your womb and bear a son and you shall name him Jesus." Now Mary was completely confused. "How can this be since I have no relations with a man?" Mary must have thought, "If this is of God, God you are not making sense yet."

"The Holy Spirit will come upon you and the power of the Most High will overshadow you." "What? This is not the way it works." Mary must have been breathless. Can we feel her head spinning with confusion?

"Therefore, the child to be born will be called Holy, the Son of God. He will be great and will be called Son of the Most High. The Lord God will give him the throne of David and his kingdom will have no end." "Is there more? Can there be any more? I cannot fathom this, Lord. I don't know what it all means and I do not understand what is happening to me."

Young Mary, we know your fear and confusion. We know you

just want to run away and hide. But don't, Mary. Please believe. Please trust. The whole world is waiting for your response, Mary. All of human history is in the balance and is hanging on what you will say. Please, Mary.

Mary said, "Behold, I am the handmaid of the Lord. May it be done to me according to your word." Mary just made the greatest act of faith and trust of all time. What can we say today? Thank you, Mary. Thank you seems hardly enough, but what more can we say?

Christmas
(Is 9:1-6; Ti 2:11-14; Lk 2:1-14)

Today we celebrate Christmas. What are we really celebrating? Given all the commercials and political correctness surrounding Christmas, I think we can almost lose the real meaning.

A Methodist pastor in South Dakota actually decided to celebrate Christmas on June 25th when people could concentrate on its real meaning without all of the distractions.

The Lutherans conducted a poll recently and found that the largest percentage of Christians said Christmas was about families getting together. Now that's an important side effect of Christmas, but what are we really celebrating?

With all due respect for other religions which celebrate special holy days at this time of the year, and I do respect them, when we celebrate Christmas we are celebrating the birth of Jesus, the Christ. I say Jesus, the Christ because Christ is not Jesus' last name. If you were to meet Jesus and his family, he would not introduce his parents like this, "Meet my mother, Mary Christ and my father, Joseph Christ." The word "Christ" means "the anointed one." It is a word used in scripture for the Messiah or Savior.

So we are celebrating Jesus' birth today, but there is so much more to Christmas than a big birthday party. We are celebrating everything his birthday meant, and that, my friends, should take our breath away.

How many of us feel loved? How many feel really loved? How many of you can say that you know a person who loves you so much that he or she would actually die for you? One of our biggest problems is that we don't feel that we are very loveable. That's why, when true love comes our way, it is a wonderful surprise.

What are we really celebrating today? We are celebrating love that should take our breath away. Now I will remind you of a few facts that we say we believe, but which demand our serious reflection. For now, forget what the Bible tells us; forget what the church has taught us. Just consider these statements at their face value.

"God Almighty, Creator of the whole universe, sent his only son to become a human being, to be born of a maiden named Mary, and to live with us on earth as one of us." Come on, Father, that sounds ridiculous. Why in the world would Almighty God do that?

"This child, born of Mary, truly human and truly God, grew up to teach us how to live, and to plead with us to believe in him, and ultimately, to endure unbelievable suffering and a cruel death nailed to a cross." Oh stop it, Father. You are dreaming, get real.

You see if the New Testament did not tell us, and if our own Church did not teach us this for 2,000 years, we would find it all fantastic and simply unbelievable. But we know it is all true, as fantastic as it sounds. Why would God do all this? For one reason only, pure love, a love so great that this God of ours sent his son to save us. God wants us to live with him forever in heaven. How big is this love? It is beyond our grasp, beyond our understanding. And God's love is not just for the whole world, for humankind in general, it is for each individual person. God loves you that way. God even loves me that way. Yes, even me. We tend to see ourselves as unlovable. It is easier for me to believe that you are loved by God in that way than it is for me to believe it about myself.

To show us how personal this love is, the great theologian St. Thomas Aquinas wrote that, "If you were the only person in human history that needed to be saved, Jesus would have been born and would have died just for you."

Christmas demands our reflection. Don't just let it slip by as another big day of the year. If we reflect, we will never again see ourselves as unlovable, we will see ourselves as the precious, loved people we are. We will be filled with gratitude and praise of God for his love, which we can never earn or deserve. If we reflect on this, we will be left breathless

The Feast of the Holy Family
(Gn 15:1-6; 21:1-3; Heb 11:8; 11-12, 17-19; Lk 2:22, 39-40)

Today is the Feast of the Holy Family. Today we honor Jesus, Mary, and Joseph as a family. Today I challenge you and myself to a difficult task. I challenge us to make this Holy Family real. What do I mean? I mean that we idolize Jesus, Mary, and Joseph to the point they cease to be real human beings like ourselves. We are so awed by the divinity of Jesus that we find it difficult to see him as a real human person. We don't totally believe Paul when he wrote, "He was like us in every way but sin." Think about that. He was human like us in every way but sin.

We honor Mary and Joseph so much that we make them out to be super human beings. We find it difficult to see them as people like us, as people involved with the questions, the stress, and the misunderstandings of real, down-to-earth life.

Let's test what I am saying. How do we picture the Holy Family? Do we see Jesus, Mary, and Joseph sitting in the living room of their spotlessly clean home praying the Psalms together, singing the praises of God in beautiful harmony? Do we see Mary as the perfect housewife and gourmet cook?

Is Joseph the ideal husband who is never too tired after a long day in the carpenter shop to help Mary with the dishes? Do we see Jesus as the perfect child, completely obedient, always ready to run errands and take out the garbage?

There is a big problem with all this. We are idealizing the Holy Family to the point that we remove them far away from the reality of our own family life. We place them on pedestals to be admired, but too far out of reach to be imitated.

Our esteem and love of the Holy Family will grow to the extent that we make them the real people they were and to the extent that we bring them closer to our own normal family life. But this is difficult. It is difficult for us to hear Mary say, "Son, don't make me tell you again to straighten out your room," or to hear Jesus asking Joseph, "Why do I have to be home by nine?"

It is difficult to hear Joseph saying, "Because I told you so."

Our gospel today invites us to the reality of their family life. It gives us a look into the hurt and misunderstanding that came with it. When Jesus was 12 years old his parents took him to the temple in Jerusalem, according to Jewish custom. They traveled to the big city with a whole caravan of relatives and acquaintances. Then the caravan returned home. Thinking he was with them, they traveled a whole day and then could not find him among their fellow travelers. Can you imagine their panic? "Where is he? Did we leave a 12-year-old boy on his own in the city? Why didn't we look for him earlier?"

With great anxiety Mary and Joseph returned to Jerusalem in search for Jesus. What were the chances of finding him at all or finding him safe and well? After three days of searching they must have been basket cases. But then they saw him sitting in the temple, unconcerned and calmly discussing his religion with the teachers. His parents were astonished. Mary said to Jesus, "Son, why have you done this to us? Your father and I have been looking for you with great anxiety." Jesus gave them a strange look and said, "Why were you looking for me? I think I have a reason to be here."

Jesus attitude must have hurt his parents even more. "Why were we looking for you?" Jesus was in his own world. He failed to see and feel the pain he had caused. The gospel stops there, but I believe that when he realized their fear and anguish he also said, "I'm really sorry, Mom and Dad." The gospel tells us that he went home to Nazareth with them and was obedient to them. Mary kept all these things in her heart as only mothers do.

Let's keep the Holy Family real. Sure, they had their hurts and misunderstandings, but there was forgiveness and reconciliation because there was love and respect in that family. If we think of them the next time we need forgiveness and reconciliation in our own family, then we will be doing more than admiring them from a distance. We will imitate them, which is the highest form of admiration.

The Feast of the Epiphany
(Is 60:1-6; Eph 3:2-3a, 5-6; Mt 2:1-12)

Today is the Feast of the Epiphany. That's a strange Greek word. What does it mean? An epiphany is a manifestation, a showing forth. An epiphany is a striking new vision. It is seeing something in a whole new way. What is the religious significance of the word "epiphany"? It means the Epiphany Star which led the first people to Jesus. But even more importantly, it means Jesus grew up to be the epiphany of God the Father. He gave a stirring new vision of God that was totally mind blowing.

Remember, the Jews saw God as an almighty, distant power who controlled their lives by obedience to his laws. The Jews were in such awe of God that they were afraid to pronounce his name, which was Yahweh. They wrote his name only with the consonants YHWH, which cannot be spoken. Then Jesus, the epiphany of God, blew their minds.

What kind of God did Jesus manifest? He taught us that God is not a distant power way off in the heavens. He told us that God is personally concerned with each one of us. God cares so much about us, in fact, that he knows the number of hairs on our heads. God loves us so much that there is nothing we could do to make God love us less. God loves us so much that he sent his only son into the world to save us. God loves us so much that he has made us part of his family. We are his sons and daughters and God wants us to be with him forever in heaven.

What a striking new revelation about God! No wonder Jesus blew the minds of his fellow Jews, and should do the same to us. Jesus was such a perfect epiphany of God. When Philip asked him to show them God the Father, Jesus said, "Philip, he who sees me sees the Father." God knows, our world today needs to know this as much as the Jewish people did 2,000 years ago. How will people know today? It will not be through another Epiphany Star in the sky. There is only one way, and it is through us. Why? Because we are the people who profess to believe in the God of Jesus. As Jesus was the epiphany of God's love in his day, you and I are the epiphany of God's love today. What kind of epiphany are we? What kind of God do we manifest? I think there is one simple test for this. It is joy. Why joy? Because it is impossible to really believe in such a God and be anything but joyful.

When people observe us what do they see? If a nonbeliever walked into church and observed us, what would he see? As people observe us at home, at work, or in our neighborhood, what do they see? Are we joyful people or not?

There is an inane song, "Don't Worry, Be Happy," that expresses a carefree attitude that puts a smile on our face when our whole life is crumbling around us. I am not talking about that kind of game or pretention. We all have problems and we get down sometimes. Sadness is a real and legitimate part of life. I am talking about our chronic condition. How are we usually? Does our faith in the God of Jesus show joy or do we show something else? Has our religion become heavy and complicated, and overwhelming in its demands? Is it so serious that it causes more frowns than smiles? Do serious and frowning people manifest a God of love? Do they lead people to a God of love?

We are epiphany today. Every moment we live we are manifesting to our world, one way or another, what kind of God we believe in. Reflect on what you believe, and smile.

The Baptism of the Lord
(Is 55:1-11; 1Jn 5:1-9; Mk 1:7-11)

Today we celebrate the baptism of the Lord.

A pastor decided to see what he could learn from Bible scholars and others about the baptism of Jesus. He went online with his computer and typed in the words, "The baptism of Jesus." Guess what he found? He found 253,000 articles, sermons, and discussions about the baptism of Jesus. He found out more than he ever wanted to know.

What do we want to know about Jesus' baptism? I will limit this homily to two questions: 1. Why was Jesus baptized if he was without sin? 2. What does Jesus' baptism have to do with our own baptism? First, why was Jesus baptized if he was without sin? John the Baptist preached a baptism of repentance for the forgiveness of sin. John knew that everyone who came to him needed to repent and needed forgiveness.

The psychiatrist Karl Menninger used to tell about two men walking down a Chicago street. Suddenly a street evangelist pointed a long, boney finger at them and shouted, "Guilty! Guilty!" One man turned to the other and said, "How did he know?" John the Baptist knew, but he also knew that the one now approaching him was not guilty. Jesus came to John and asked to be baptized. John hesitated. He said to Jesus, "I need to be baptized by you." "No," Jesus said, "It is to fulfill all righteousness."

So John baptized Jesus and, as Jesus came out of the water he heard a voice from heaven say, "You are my beloved son. With you I am well pleased." What did Jesus mean, "To fulfill all righteousness"? Bible scholars say it has to do with Jesus' special relationship to God and his firm commitment to do God's will. Jesus was saying to God and to the world what he said later in the Garden of Gethsemane, "Not what I will, but what you will."

Second, what is the link between the baptism of Jesus and our own baptism? Our baptism is about our special relationship with God and our firm commitment to do God's will. Most of us were too young to remember our baptism but our parents and godparents made that commitment for us. Here are the exact words: The priest asks, "Parents, what do you ask of God's Church for your child?" The parents respond, "Baptism." The priest continues, "You have asked to have your child baptized. In doing so you are accepting the responsibility of training him in the practice of the faith. It will be your duty to bring him up to keep God's commandments as Christ taught us, by loving God and our neighbor. Do you clearly understand what you are undertaking?" The parents respond, "We do." Then the priest addresses the godparents, "Godparents, are you ready to help these parents in their duty as Christian mothers and fathers?" The godparents respond, "We are."

Our baptism was the beginning of a special relationship to God, and it was the moment when we were committed to do the Father's will. And, although no voice was heard from Heaven, at our baptism God said to us, "You are my beloved child; with you I am well pleased." We are God's sons and daughters. As Paul wrote, "With Christ we are God's children and heirs of heaven. And it all began when we were baptized just as Jesus was baptized.

We need to reflect on our baptism. Do not think too little of yourself. Yes, we are special people. Yes, we are dedicated people. Yes, we are committed people. And every time we do the Father's will, God says again to us, "You are my beloved child; with you I am well pleased."

In my baptism classes I ask parents why they want their children baptized. Quite often, I get the answer, "I want God to bless my baby." My friends, baptism is much more than a blessing. It made us God's beloved children. We were changed forever.

The Second Sunday of the Year
(1 Sam 3:3b-10, 19; 1 Cor 6:13c-15a, 17-20; Jn 1:35-42)

Today's readings are about the call and answering the call. Today we are so anxious to get every call that we walk around with our cell phones. Everywhere we go our cell phone goes with us so we won't miss a single call. I'm sure cell phones are a valuable invention but sometimes they drive me nuts. Do cell phones irritate you? It irritates me to see a driver with a phone to his ear. I feel like saying, "Put the darn phone down and drive with both your hands."

When my friend, Fr. Padilla and I were in San Diego recently we went to a movie. Not one, but two phones rang and people just had to take their calls. As anxious as we seem to be to answer every call, I suggest today that there is a little phone inside each of us and it rings frequently, but we hesitate to answer it.

Today's readings are about the call and answering the call. In our first reading God called Samuel several times but he did not understand who was calling. Then Eli helped Samuel to understand. So when God called again, "Samuel, Samuel," Samuel answered, "Speak, Lord, for your servant is listening."

In our gospel Jesus saw Andrew and another disciple following him and asked them, "What are you looking for?" They said to him, "Rabbi, where are you staying?" And Jesus called them, "Come, and you will see. Come, and you will see where I am staying. You will see what I am all about by four o'clock this afternoon."

Now, when we talk about a call from God, "call" becomes a very powerful word. It evokes feelings of being special and singled out by God. How privileged Samuel and Andrew were to be called by God and Jesus.

Let's stop thinking about them or about other people. What about us? Are we privileged? I said we all have a little phone inside us and God is on the line. God's call may be a little nudging, an insight, or an idea that keeps popping up inside. These are the kind that makes us wonder, "Now where did that come from?"

Do you believe this? You might answer, "Oh, maybe you do, but not me." Not you? Come on! There are only two possibilities. Let's look at them. First, if God is not calling you that means God has either given up on you or is completely satisfied with you the way you are now. How does this set with you? It doesn't sound right, does it? We know God does not give up on anyone. We know God is not satisfied with us now when our potential is so much greater. The second possibility is that God is calling you and me. Just like Samuel and Andrew, God is calling us to much more. God has big plans for us. God is calling us to be our very best. God is calling us to true holiness. How does this set with you? We know in our heart that it is true. I know I am speaking to every single one of us here. No one can say, "I don't know what you are talking about, Father." We know inside.

If we know, then why do we hesitate to answer those interior calls? We might say, "I don't understand what God is calling me to." Neither did Samuel, but he answered his call, "Speak Lord, for your servant is listening."

All God wants us to do is answer his phone call. Don't pretend God is not calling. Don't think God has the wrong number. Don't put God on hold. Don't give God the busy signal.

We do not have to be afraid to answer. Wherever God is calling us to be is the right place for us. God loves us so much; he wants only the best for us. God will never call us to anything less. All we need to do is answer, "Speak Lord, for your servant is listening." If we answer that way, it will lead us to the peace and joy that only God can give us.

The Third Sunday of the Year
(Jon 3:1-5, 10; 1 Cor 7:29-31; Mk 1:14-20)

We place special importance on first words and last words. My mother kept a baby book on me. Do mothers still do that? On page 7 are Bobbie's first words, spoken at ten months. They were not very original first words: "Papa" and "Mama," with the notation, "But he may not know what he is saying."

Last words have special importance. There is a saying that "you can always believe the words of a dying person."

In today's gospel Mark records the first words that Jesus spoke in his public life. What are they? "This is the time of fulfillment. The kingdom of heaven is at hand. Repent and believe in the Gospel."

Last week we talked about the little phone inside each of us and about God calling us in our hearts. Today we have a different kind of call, a general call to all of us. Jesus calls all of us frequently in the gospels. He calls us to repent and to believe.

What does it mean to you to repent? It may mean something

different to you than to me. Here's where the little phone inside helps us to make this general call into a personal call. However, there are certain basics that will guide all of us in understanding Jesus' call to repent.

What is our religious life? What is our faith life? Is our religion basically a list of teachings? Our teachings are important, but Jesus' call to repent is much deeper than any creed or formula of faith. Remember, the apostles died long before there was an Apostle's Creed. Is our religious life basically a set of rules and laws? Rules and laws we must have, but Jesus' call to repent goes much deeper than any code of conduct.

The real meaning of Jesus' call is found in the original Greek word for repent, "metanoia," which means "a complete change of mind and heart." "Metanoia" means getting underneath the surface, underneath our spiritual routines, underneath our dogmas and rules and getting to the heart of the matter, which is our heart.

Jesus calls us to a basic change of heart and mind; to a major reshaping of our values, perspective, and attitude, and to change not just what we do, but who we are. For example, when we examine our consciences we concentrate on our thoughts, words, and actions. But we usually stop there. Our thoughts, words, and actions are important, but more importantly, they are signs that point to what kind of people we are. Jesus calls us to go beyond what we do to the more important question of who we are.

Obviously, if we are doing things we know are wrong, we need to repent of those things. But that is just the start. We need to look at the bigger picture of ourselves. What kind of person am I? What am I really after in life? Am I basically a selfish, self-centered person or one who is directed outward to others? Am I more materialistically than spiritually oriented? To what extent does greed influence my life? Is pride, self-seeking, and the admiration of others a big part of everything I do?

Those are some of the bigger questions Jesus calls us to consider. Can we answer such questions? We can and we will if we keep answering that interior phone. God does not call us to the impossible. God is in charge of our spiritual growth. God knows who we are and what we need and will make it all happen if we listen to our hearts and keep responding, "Speak Lord, for your servant is listening."

The Fourth Sunday of the Year
(Dt 18:15-20; 1 Cor 7:32-35; Mk 1:21-28)

Our big word today is "authority." A few years ago a man approached me. He was terribly excited about some revelations given to a religious woman. In fact, she had so many revelations that they filled up several volumes. He insisted that I must read them. I told him, "I'm sure it's all very interesting and it probably satisfies our curiosity to know more than the gospels tell us, but, no thank you." I know the gospels are the inspired word of God. I feel more than challenged by Jesus in the gospels, and the gospels speak with authority that no private revelation has.

On another occasion, a woman whom I had never met came to the office and delivered to me two whole new gospels someone had discovered. They were full of new parables and stories about Jesus. She too insisted that I must read them. Once again, I told her that I was not interested because our four gospels speak with authority no others have.

Our gospel today speaks about authority. The people were astonished because Jesus taught with authority. All were amazed and asked, "What is this? A new teaching with authority and even unclean spirits obey him."

Webster defines "authority" as the power to influence thought and behavior. Our questions today are: 1. Does Jesus have authority in our lives? 2. Is it Jesus who influences our thought and behavior or is it some other authority?

Let's look at a few examples:

1. Governmental Authority

Now I do not intend to be political. I have no desire to debate any of these examples. I propose them as philosophical questions. How much of our thought and behavior is influenced by governmental authority? Do we accept legislated morality? When government rules that abortion is allowed, because it is legal, does that make it moral? When government tells us that capital punishment is appropriate for certain crimes, does that make it morally acceptable? When the Supreme Court rules that the state of Oregon can allow assisted suicide, does that ruling make it okay? When government legislates a minimum wage of $7.25 an hour, does that make the wage fair and just compensation? Remember, our questions are: Who has authority in our lives? And, how much does governmental authority influence our thought and behavior?

2. Social Authority

Social authority means the powerful pressures that society

imposes on our thought and behavior. Society calls us to success and to money, and to the power and influence that money can give us. Society tells us that we had better stay in step with our competitors if we are going to survive. If everyone else is doing it, that is, cutting corners, stepping on others, and doing away with retirement plans, then we must do it too in order to stay competitive.

A business executive told me that competition is so fierce that business ethics must be legislated because no one can afford to take the first step and be the nice guy or he will be gobbled up by the competition. Our questions are: Who has authority in our lives? How much does society with its goals and rewards influence our thoughts and behavior?

3. Peer Authority

Peer Authority means the powerful pressures from our peers, especially those placed on our young people. Peer pressure on our young people in school is enormous. Peer pressure says, "Don't be different. Go along with what most are doing. If you dare to be different you will be on the outs, and who wants that? So, once again, who has authority in our lives? How much does peer pressure influence our thought and behavior?

Jesus taught with authority. Jesus wants authority in our lives. Sometimes Jesus speaks to us very differently than government, society, or peers, or any other group. When we hear conflicting authorities, whose authority do we follow? There are many voices, loud voices, screaming for our attention. Among those voices is Jesus who insists that he must be the one who has the power to influence our thought and behavior. Do we hear him?

📖 The Fifth Sunday of the Year
(Jb 7:1-4, 6-7; 1 Cor 9:16-19, 22-23; Mk 1:29-39)

Week after week we listen to the gospels. Week after week we hear what Jesus did and said. Today's gospel is what scripture scholars call a summary statement about the whole ministry of Jesus. It summarizes what he was all about.

"They brought to him all who were ill and Jesus healed them."

"Everyone was looking for him."

"Let us go on to nearby villages that I may preach the Good News there also. For this purpose have I come."

So there's our summary statement about Jesus: loving people, caring for people, healing people, teaching people the good news about God and his kingdom.

As we listen to these gospels week after week, do we ever think, "Wouldn't it have been great to have lived in one of these nearby villages, to have heard the words of Jesus as he spoke them, and to have been touched by Jesus in a healing way?" But we were not there. The reality is we live now, not 2,000 years ago. So are we the less fortunate ones? Are we deprived in some way because we were not there? In no way. Why do I say that? It is because Jesus is alive and well today. Jesus said he would be with us always. He knows each one of us as well as he knew anyone 2,000 years ago. Jesus loves each one of us as he loved anyone when he was on earth. He continues to heal us as he healed them. He continues to preach his good news to us week after week, every time we read the scriptures.

What I hope to do in this homily is to keep us from falling into some kind of nostalgia about the Jesus who was. I want us to realize that Jesus is just as real and present to us today, and to have us move from an admiration of a Jesus who lived in past history, to a realization of his love, his presence, and his power in our lives right now. So I ask you, what has Jesus done for you? What is Jesus doing for you now? How is Jesus touching you in healing ways now? I cannot answer that for you. I will answer it for myself, and I encourage you to answer for yourself.

I just finished reading a book about the priesthood. The author wrote about different kinds of priests, about how priests are trained, and about how priests have changed from pre-Vatican II days until now. The book made me reflect over more than fifty years of my life as a priest. I reflected on how I used to be and how I am now, as well as on what I could have been but did not become. And POW! It was like a light bulb turned on in my head. I was overcome by the marvels Jesus had done in my life. Oh, I am not saying I have arrived. God knows I have a long way to go. I am not finished yet. Jesus needs to keep working with me to make me a better priest, but I absolutely marvel at what God has done and continues to do in me. God is almost unbelievable, almost too good to be true.

I tell you this because I want you to see the wonderful things God has done for you. I want you to marvel about yourself, and to make Jesus just as real in your life as he was to Peter, Andrew, James, John, Peter's mother-in-law, and all the people whom he touched.

So I ask you again, what has Jesus done for you? What is Jesus doing for you now? How is Jesus touching you in healing ways? How are you a different person today than you were five years ago? How have your attitudes and your values changed? How differently do you see things now than you did five or ten years ago?

Go with it and you will feel closer to Jesus because Jesus is more real to you. You will be filled with awe over the power of Jesus in your life. You will be filled with wonder and gratitude knowing how much Jesus must love you to work such marvels in you.

📖 The Sixth Sunday of the Year
(Lv 13:1-2, 44-46; 1 Cor 10:31, 11:1; Mk 1:40-45)

Today's gospel makes me want to talk about prayer. Why? It is because prayer is important to us. We all pray. Although the word "prayer" is not mentioned in today's gospel, I think this gospel is telling us something important about prayer. Let's look at what our gospel tells us and let's look at how we pray.

A leper came to Jesus and, kneeling down before him, begged him, "If you wish you can make me clean." There are two important elements in his prayer. When the leper says, "If you wish," he is saying, "Not as I want so desperately, but as you wish." He is saying, "I trust your will, Jesus. I trust that you want only the best for me. You know what is best for me and you will give me only the best. "The leper's prayer is full of faith and confidence. He did not say, "Maybe you can make me clean." He said, "I know you can make me clean. I have no doubt. I know you can."

Jesus stretched out his hand, touched the leper and said, "I do will it. Be made clean." Throughout the gospels it is the same story. Jesus responded to prayer that was made with real faith and confidence. "Your faith has saved you." How many times have we heard that in the gospels?

Dr. Edward Bosworth was a professor at a seminary in Ohio. He was known to be a man of deep prayer. A man, whose daughter Mary was having problems, wrote to Dr. Bosworth asking him to include Mary among those for whom he prayed each day. The man received an immediate reply in which Dr. Bosworth expressed his concern for Mary. But he said it was impossible for him to include Mary on his prayer list because the list was already full. Dr. Bosworth wrote, "I don't think I should have more people on my list than I can attend to thoughtfully and prayerfully. A person must mean business with all the powers of his mind and spirit when he lifts another person in prayer to God. When there is a vacancy on my list, I will include Mary." Now, we may not agree with Dr. Bosworth's decision, but we cannot doubt his conviction that we must mean business when we pray.

Lots of people ask me to pray for them or other people in need. I tell them I will place them in my prayer bundle. The bundle is pretty big. So whenever I celebrate Mass or pray the Liturgy of the Hours or the Rosary, I say to the Lord, "I present to you my bundle." I cannot remember each name or specific need, but I know God knows all of that and accepts my prayer bundle. I hope that does not mean that I do not take prayer seriously like Dr. Bosworth. I believe that I do take those requests seriously. I do not say that my prayer bundle cannot take on another person because I believe that

God's mercy and love are much bigger than my bundle.

Now let's look at how we pray. Do we take prayer seriously? Do we mean business when we pray or could we describe our prayer as casual or half-hearted? Is prayer our first resort? Is it made with confidence and faith or is it our last resort as in, "I've tried everything else, all I can do now is pray." Do we pray convinced that God hears us and wants only the best for us or do we pray as if God does not really care and does not really want to help us? Do we pray without really expecting anything to happen? And, if something does happen, are we surprised? Do we say, "Oh my God, I prayed for something and it worked!"

"If you wish you can make me clean. I truly believe you can. I have full confidence you can. Will you?" "I will do it. Be made clean."

The Seventh Sunday of the Year
(Is 43:18-19, 21-22, 24b-25; 2 Cor 1:18-22; Mk 2:1-12)

Our scriptures today are about God's forgiveness. So today I speak only to the sinners among us. The rest of you may take a short nap. But don't any of you start to nod. Why? Because there is no one among us who hasn't at some point needed forgiveness. We are all sinners and we all need forgiveness over and over again. That's why theologian Morton Kelsey wrote that the church "…is not a museum for saints, but a hospital for sinners."

How do we deal with our sinfulness? In my years as a priest I have been saddened countless times by people who carry the burden of their past sins, sometimes to the grave. Oh sure, we will never forget our sins and the ways we have hurt people, but remembering our sins is very different from carrying them around as a burden. The fear, disappointment, sadness, and guilt over the past can paralyze us spiritually. We create our own roadblock in our relationship with God and other people. This kind of guilt is hurting us.

I believe healthy guilt is something like this. When we recall past sins we can make it an occasion for praying, "Lord, have mercy on me, a sinner. Lord, I see how I can do nothing right without you." And then we move on with our life. But this presumes that we really believe God has forgiven us.

Let's look at God's word to see how God forgives us. In our gospel, the paralytic was brought to Jesus for physical healing. Jesus saw that spiritual healing was even more important. Spiritual paralysis needed to be dealt with more urgently than physical paralysis.

"Child, your sins are forgiven." The Scribes objected, "He is blaspheming. Who but God alone can forgive sin?" And the Scribes were correct. Sure, we can forgive others who have hurt us. We might even be able to forgive ourselves. But the evil of sin itself only God can forgive. Jesus responded, "But that you may know that the Son of Man has authority to forgive sins," he said to the paralytic, "rise, pick up your mat, and go home."

Throughout the gospels we see Jesus forgiving people. In Luke 7, a woman who had a bad reputation weeps at the feet of Jesus. How does Jesus deal with her? He did not lecture her or cross examine her. He did not shake his head and say, "My, my, how could you have done this?" Jesus did not say that she should feel guilty for the rest of her life. He said to her, "Your sins are forgiven. Go in peace."

That's how Jesus dealt with sinful people, not just by forgiving them but by wiping the slate clean. We may have a hard time letting go of our sins, but Jesus does not. They are gone forever. His forgiveness gives people a fresh start. We truly begin again as new people. So be at peace.

Do we really believe that? Well, if this is not enough, listen to God in our first reading from Isaiah, "You burdened me with your sins and wearied me with your crimes. It is I who wipe out your offences, your sins I remember no more." When God forgives us, in God's mind it is as if it never happened. Now that is complete forgiveness.

Listen to the prophet Micah, "God will have compassion upon us. He will tread our iniquities underfoot. God will cast all our sins into the depths of the sea." That means that God won't haul up our sins from the bottom of the sea, and neither should we.

Lord, we thank you and praise you for your total and compassionate forgiveness. Help us to believe more firmly in your forgiveness.

The Eighth Sunday of the Year
(Hos 2:16b, 17b, 21-22; 2 Cor 3:1-6; Mk 2:18-22)

Listen to Jesus in today's gospel. "No one sews a piece of unshrunken cloth on an old cloak. If he does, its fullness pulls away, the new from the old, and the tear gets worse. Likewise, no one pours new wine into old wineskins. Otherwise, the wine will burst the skins and both the wine and the skins are ruined. Rather, new wine is poured into fresh wineskins."

That may sound strange and, as we reflect on it, it can even get scary. Jesus' teaching was new wine. It was different from the slavish obedience to laws that the Pharisees taught. Jesus taught that love and human need sometimes take precedence over laws. For these reasons Jesus even broke some religious laws. His teaching was so new and different that the religious leaders could not tolerate it and Jesus' new wine ultimately led to his death.

In our gospel today, those people who were threatened by what was new are the old cloaks and wineskins. But that was then. How about now? Are there any old cloaks and wineskins among us? Another way of asking the question is, are there any among us who are so afraid of the new and unknown that we resist change? Change of any kind creates something new and uncertain. I think we all resist change to one degree or other. There is an old saying, "The only person who welcomes change is a wet baby." Let's put it yet another way. Are we so set in our ways and so comfortable with things as they are, that we resist change? There is a certain security with keeping things the same and a corresponding insecurity with changing them. Are we holding on so tightly that we are not open to God's promptings within us to step out of our comfort zone?

These are important questions as we approach the beginning of Lent. Why? It is because Lent is all about change. Lent is God's call to conversion and to change of heart in very deep ways. Lent is a call to become new people, and that can sound a little scary.

Today's gospel is getting closer and very personal to each one of us. But this call to become new people is not a new call. It is the heart of our Christian faith. Christianity is not something that is meant to be tacked on to life as it is. It is a call to new life. It is the heart of Jesus' teaching. Does not Jesus call us to faith, to deep faith in God, even though we cannot see where it might take us? Does not Jesus call us to absolute trust in God's love for us? So, wherever God leads us may be new, but it does not have to be scary.

As we begin Lent, we have a basic choice to make. We can live Lent on the surface, we can do a little fasting, say a few extra prayers, and maybe give up something or deny ourselves in some way, but this makes Lent a dull, gray time of year. Or we can approach Lent with a mind and heart open to whatever God wants for us, with faith and trust that God leads us in love. This makes Lent a joyful and exciting time of year.

📖 The First Sunday of Lent
(Gn 9:8-15; 1 Pt 3:18-22; Mk 1:12-15)

Jesus experienced the first Lent. The spirit drove Jesus out into the desert and he remained in the desert for 40 days, tempted by Satan. His temptation took him right to the heart of the matter.

Jesus had lived for thirty years in relative quiet and obscurity. He lived a very ordinary life working as a carpenter. Now his time had come. It was time for Jesus to deal with who he really was. It was time for him to wrestle with his identity, with what he was really about, and with what his Father wanted of him.

Jesus was facing a critical time in his life. It was a time of passage from the life he knew to a dramatically different life. He would pass from a private person to a public person. He would become a leader of people, not the kind of leader Satan tempted him to be, not the kind of leader people wanted him to be, that is, a charismatic and powerful leader who would restore Israel to its glory days, but a leader who would take a very different road.

Can we imagine spending forty days in this kind of soul-searching, questioning, coming to awareness, and taking action from that awareness? Can we imagine such a time when we face ourselves for who we really are, what we are really about, and what we will do about it?

We know where Jesus' Lent brought him. Jesus came out of the desert proclaiming God's good news, "This is the time of fulfillment. The Reign of God is at hand. Repent and believe the good news." Jesus came out of the desert knowing who he was and knowing what he must be about, and was totally committed to that, no matter where it would lead him. Jesus had a powerful Lenten experience and he is calling us to have the same.

These next forty days are our "time of fulfillment." It is our time to sift through the nonessentials of our life and get to the heart of the matter. If we are concerned about what we will give up this Lent, we are not dealing with the heart of the matter. Discipline yourself anyway you wish, but let's remember that the purpose of discipline is to free us and focus us on the heart of the matter.

What is the heart of the matter? Who are you? Who am I? What are we really about? What are we really after in life? Do I want the next ten years of my life to be a repetition of the last ten? Or do I want it to be different? Different how? What does God really want from me? Who is God calling me to become? And what will I do about this?

These are tough questions to deal with. That's why we keep putting them off. But they won't go away. They have to be dealt with sooner or later. People who avoid them during their earlier years have them come crashing down hard later. These people will experience severe mid-life crises. People who put these questions on hold through most of their lives find themselves in that scary situation of having to deal with them at the end of life. Jesus is calling us to deal with these questions now, no matter what our age may be. If we do it now, we too will find that awareness and that ability to distinguish what really counts from the trivial of life.

Thank God for Lent. This is our time of fulfillment. Lent is a special time, a blessed time, and we need it to confront the heart of the matter. With God's help we will be different people come Easter. With God's help we will come out of our desert experience like Jesus did, totally committed to God's call wherever it leads us.

The Second Sunday of Lent
(Gn 22:1-2, 9a, 10-13, 15-18; Rom 8:31b-34; Mk 9:2-10)

Today is the Feast of Transfiguration. The dictionary tells us that to transfigure is to change so as to glorify. Peter, James, and John had a glimpse of Jesus who was more than he seemed to be. It was a glimpse of Jesus in his glory. His clothes became so white that they dazzled them. Peter barely knew what to say, they were all so terrified. What a moment this was for Peter, James, and John.

Have you ever had a glimpse of yourself and discovered that you were more than you seemed to be? I don't mean that you appeared in glory like you will in heaven. I mean a moment of insight and clarity when you realized you were more than you thought you were. Have you ever had a glimpse of your life when you realized that your life was part of something much bigger than yourself?

Perhaps the most difficult part of our lives is the repetition and routine that pervades everyday living. We are surrounded with sameness. There are one thousand little things we need to do over and over just to survive. When we load the dishwasher we know we'll do it again soon. When we dust the furniture we know it won't last long. When we shave we know those darn whiskers will be back tomorrow. There really is no closure on the one thousand little things that make up so much of our lives. No wonder we get into ruts, it's just more of the same. No wonder we sometimes question what it's all about and what it all adds up to.

You and I need some transfiguration experiences. We need to see ourselves as more than that. We need to see our lives as more than that. We have those moments. They are there. We need to recognize them. Here are a few examples from my life.

An active Catholic who had not darkened a church door for many years darkened our doors because he was attending the funeral of a friend. He was so moved by the whole thing that he told a parishioner he was seriously thinking of returning to church. Lord, your grace is really powerful. My life is part of something much bigger than myself.

Sometime between 2 and 3 a.m. the phone rings. A dying man wanted the Last Rites. Now, at 2 to 3 a.m. my initial response is not always my best me. Of course I said yes, but inside I said to myself, "Why couldn't they have called me yesterday? Why do they wait to the last minute?" But I was okay by the time I got to the man's house. I gave him the Last Rites. As I was walking out I heard him say to his son, "He is my savior." I am his savior? No way, Lord, you are his savior. But it made me reflect on what an awesome thing it is to help prepare someone for death. What an unearned privilege it is for me to do that. It was a transfiguration moment and on the way home I thanked God for waking me sometime between 2 and 3 a.m.

A person comes to this church for the first time and after Mass says to me, "Thank you, Father; you were speaking right to me today." Lord, what does this mean?

You might say, "Sure, Father, those things happen to you because you are a priest, but they don't happen to me." Oh yes they do. We all have transfiguration moments. Consider how the routine and sameness of life fades when a new parent holds a baby and looks into those eyes and counts those little fingers. Lord, this baby is part of me. Consider how an elderly person can look into the eyes of a spouse, without a word being spoken, and can be overwhelmed by the love they have shared for so many years. Consider how someone can tell you how much you have done for them by a simple word or gesture and you wonder, "Who, me? I had no idea." Consider how in a rare moment of quiet you are filled with a peaceful sense of God's presence and you just know it is all true. God is real, God does love you, and you will live with God forever. Consider how you can reflect on your own life, everything that has happened and not happened, and suddenly you are aware of how Jesus has saved you from so much, and how Jesus has walked with you every step of the way. All you can say is WOW!

Sure our lives are filled with one thousand things we do over and over again just to survive. Every once in a while, however, we ascend the mountain of transfiguration. Every once in a while we have a glimpse of ourselves as more than we seem to be. Along with Peter we say, "Master, how good it is for us to be here." Treasure these moments.

The Third Sunday of Lent
(Ex 20:1-17; 1 Cor 1:22-25; Jn 2:13-25)

When I read the gospel in preparation for my homilies I sometimes think that whoever chooses the gospel reading has never been a priest and has never had to give a homily about it. That's how I felt when I read today's gospel. An angry Jesus used a whip to drive the sellers and money changers out of the temple. He turned over their tables and spilled their coins all over the pavement. Obviously, this is a picture of an angry Jesus, but what does it have to do with us today?

After some reflection part of this gospel spoke to me. "Jesus knew them all and did not need anyone to testify about human nature. He himself understood it well." This certainly speaks to you and me. Jesus knows us all very well. He knows our hearts and understands our human nature well. So our question today is this. If Jesus came to our church, would he throw you out? Would he throw me out? Why would Jesus object to us being in our church? We are not selling animals or changing money. But as Jesus looks into our hearts, what does he see?

We are here in church to participate in Mass, to ritualize our faith in Jesus and our love for God and one another. That's wonderful if Jesus sees that our hearts are in what we are doing. But Jesus cannot stand mere externalism in ritual or going through the motions without our hearts being in it. Why are we here? Are we here because we think we have to be here? Would we rather be somewhere else, and are here only because we are obliged to be here? Why are we here? Are we resigned to going through another boring ritual because the Church says we should be here?

Do you see what we are doing? "I am here to worship you, Lord, because I have to. I join this Mass of praise and thanksgiving because I am obligated to praise you and thank you." It's like little Suzie who fought with her daddy before he left for work. Her mommy told her, "When Daddy comes home you go up to him and tell him you love him, and that's an order." Suzie goes to her daddy and says, "Daddy, I love you. Mommy made me say this." Well, her daddy did not feel loved at all. God does not feel praised or thanked when people do it out of obligation.

We are here in church now to participate in Mass, but do we really believe God's word that we hear? Do we honestly try to live God's word every day? When we engage in religious ritual without really taking God's word to heart and living it, then this ritual of holiness itself becomes a mask of unholiness.

In the season of Lent God's word is very clear, "Reform your lives and believe in the gospel." We are halfway through Lent. What is happening to us? Let me give you an example. When we apply for Social Security we use our best earning quarters to count for our retirement. Spiritually, would we choose the last three weeks as the ones to count for our eternity? If not, why not? What was lacking? Have we not yet taken the gospel seriously? Have we not yet gotten serious about reforming our lives and changing our hearts?

I think today's gospel was assigned to the third Sunday of Lent for a reason. It's like Jesus is saying to us, "Please take me seriously. Take my life and death seriously. Take my love seriously. Don't play games with me. Games make me angry. This is your time of fulfillment. The kingdom of God is near you. Reform your lives and change your hearts, and believe in the gospel."

Our time of fulfillment is half over. Let's put our hearts into making the second half of Lent the best effort we can make because we know this is precious time, and because we take Jesus seriously.

📖 The Fourth Sunday of Lent
(2 Chr 36:14-16, 19-23; Eph 2:4-10; Jn 3:14-21)

The fourth Sunday of Lent is called Laetare Sunday. That comes from the Latin "to rejoice or be joyful." We need Laetare Sunday when we look at all the sadness and suffering in our world today. There are wars and threats of wars, poverty and denial of human rights. We need to rejoice in something and today Jesus and St. Paul give us good reason to rejoice.

When we watch football games we've all seen that character in the end zone with orange, blue, and purple hair, holding up a sign that reads simply, "John 3:16." John 3:16 is probably the best known line from the Bible and it is in our gospel today. John 3:16 says, "For God so loved the world that he gave his only son so that everyone who believes in him might not perish but have eternal life."

That's good news! And Jesus continues and makes it even better, "For God did not send his son into the world to condemn the world, but that the world might be saved through him." Today Jesus is saying, "Rejoice. I have come not to condemn but to save. Everyone who believes in me will have eternal life." That's you and I.

In our second reading Paul tells us, "For by grace you have been saved. This is not from you; it is the gift of God. It is not from our works or merits so that no one may boast. It is the gift of God." Now isn't that something that should make us jump with joy? Ah, but as good as it sounds, it is difficult for us to accept it and believe it. It sort of goes against our grain because we are not used to accepting pure gift. We believe that we need to earn it or deserve it in some way. We feel uncomfortable when somebody gives us a very expensive Christmas present and we give only a token gift back. It is hard to accept a gift without reciprocating in some way, making things equal. If a complete stranger gave you a $100 bill wouldn't you be suspicious? How can you give me $100 when I have done nothing to earn it? And if the stranger said he gave it to you just because he wanted to, and because he thought you were a nice person, you would probably call a cop.

This is a true story. A man who inherited millions of dollars decided to give it all away. He was going to until some of his relatives convinced a judge that he was insane and had him locked up. People just don't do such things. We bring this same attitude to our personal relationships. We hear expressions like, "He's never done anything to be my friend." Or, "After all I've done for her, I deserve better than that." We bring this same attitude to God. We insist we are worthy or unworthy of God's love. If we get to heaven, we have earned it. History has shown our tendency to slip back into a theology of righteousness. We believe that we can somehow affect God's love for us by what we do. How dare Paul tell us we are saved only by the grace of God! How dare Paul tell us it is not from us or from our works. It is a gift of God. See how our good news can go against our grain?

My friends, this is Rejoice Sunday! Let us just let go of all that stuff. "But…but…" No more buts! Let us simply rejoice because God so loved us he gave us his only son. Jesus came not to condemn, but to save us. Everyone who believes in Jesus will have eternal life. Let us just believe Jesus and accept this wonderful gift without feeling we have to earn it. Let us just admit that we could never do anything to merit such love from God, and we could never do anything to deserve an eternity of happiness with God. Let us just jump for joy over being loved so much and just live as people who are so loved. Oh, how our lives will change when we come to believe and accept this truth.

📖 The Fifth Sunday of Lent
(Jer 31:31-34; Heb 5:7-9; Jn 12:20-33)

"I say to you, unless a grain of wheat falls to the ground and dies, it remains just a grain of wheat. But if it dies, it produces much fruit."

Next Sunday is Palm Sunday, the beginning of Holy Week. We have only two weeks of Lent left. In today's gospel Jesus is feeling that his time has come, that his life is about to end. "I am troubled now. Yet what should I say? Father, save me from this hour. But it was for this purpose that I came to this hour. When I am lifted up, I will draw everyone to myself."

Jesus is the grain of wheat that will die to produce life in us. Today Jesus asks us to do the same. "Whoever serves me must follow me." What are we saying? Jesus is asking us to die? Yes, he is, but we need to explain that. All during Lent we have been talking about focusing on the heart of the matter rather than the nonessential, like what we are giving up for Lent. The heart of the matter is us. What kind of people are we and what are we all about?

We know in our hearts that we are still very incomplete and unfinished. We know we have a lot of potential that has not yet been realized. Jesus is calling us to take the next step and reach the next level. We cannot do that without dying to ourselves in some way. Let's take a hint from a Peanuts comic strip. Linus finds his older, crabby sister, Lucy, crying bitterly. "Mom promised me a birthday party and now I can't have one." Linus, in his quiet, wise way offers this advice, "You are not using the right strategy. Why not go up to Mom and say to her, 'I'm sorry, dear Mother. I admit I have been bad. You were right to cancel my party. But from now on I will try to be good.'" Lucy thinks about it. She prepares her speech to her mother, then she thinks about it some more. Then the stubborn Lucy cries out, "I'd rather die." Lucy could not die to her stubbornness, self-will, and pride in order to achieve her goal. Now, let's look at ourselves.

Why do we seem to be stuck where we are? What will it take to move us to this next level? From Jesus' death came new life. From our death to self in some way, we will come to new life. What is there in me that I must die to in order to move on? What must I let go of to respond fully to the Lord's call? What am I hanging onto that I'm afraid to let go of?

Let's look inside to see what might be there. Am I afraid to let go of something? Am I afraid to turn it over to the Lord because he might take it away? Am I clinging to the image of success because I don't think I could live with failure? Are possessions and financial security so important to me because I can't stand the thought of any change in my lifestyle? Am I clinging to what other people think of me, wondering whether they like me or respect me? Do I find myself promoting myself and my image in everything I do? Am I living compromised in some way? Is there something in my life that will not stand the test of the gospel? Do I hesitate to look Jesus in the eye? Why do I hesitate? What do I have to let go of and die to? Can I say, "Yes, Lord, I am ready to follow you wherever you wish to take me?

I know these are tough questions for you and me. Tough because it is hard to die, tough because it is hard to let go and trust the Lord. But let's remember, the Lord, who wants our trust, is the Lord who became the grain of wheat that died so that we may live. How can we not trust him?

📖 Palm Sunday

Picture the scene. Jesus is about to enter Jerusalem mounted on a donkey. A huge crowd greeted him. They spread their cloaks on the road. They cut branches from the trees and laid them along his path. The crowd kept crying out, "Hosanna to the Son of David. Blessed is he who comes in the name of the Lord. Hosanna in the highest." As he entered Jerusalem, the whole city was stirred to its depths.

If we might use a modern phrase, Jesus had his fifteen minutes of fame and glory, but he did not revel in it. He knew what was waiting for him in the city: suffering and death. He knew the huge crowd that was cheering him as the Son of David would, in a few days, be shouting "Crucify him!" As John 2:25 states, "Jesus would not trust himself to them because he knew them all. He needed no one to give him testimony about human nature. He was well aware of what was in man's heart."

Today our Church is calling us to walk with Jesus rather than abandoning him. We are called to walk with him through

Holy Thursday and through the horrors of Good Friday. Remember, Jesus did all of this for us in order to bring us to his glorious resurrection on Easter morning and to our own resurrection to new life that will never end.

Can Jesus trust himself to us?

(Holy Thursday and Good Friday homilies are in year A)

📖 Easter
(Acts 10:34a, 37-43; Col 3:1-4; Jn 20:1-9)

I want to tell you a true story about a woman named Pat. She came upon an old lady selling spring flowers on a street corner on Easter Sunday. Picture the flower lady as Pat saw her. The flower lady was so thin that the word "frail" did not seem strong enough to describe her. Her face was wrinkled and bronzed by too much time in the sun. Her grey hair was pinned up in a bun and covered with a funny, little hat with fake flowers on it. Her clothes were too big and well-worn. Can you see her?

As Pat approached her she saw her face. It was absolutely radiant and smiling. It was the kind of smile that made her look beautiful. Taking a flower, Pat paid her and said to her, "How happy you look this morning." Pat was not prepared for the flower lady's response, "Everything is beautiful!" "What?" Seeing her obvious condition in life, Pat thought, how could everything be beautiful? Pat said to the flower lady, "You certainly wear your troubles well."

Still beaming with a big smile, the flower lady really startled Pat by saying, "When Jesus died on Good Friday that was the worst of days. Then three days later came Easter. So when troubles come my way, I simply wait three days and trust, then everything gets all right again."

The flower lady was a very good theologian. Without knowing it, she captured the real meaning of Holy Week and Easter. She knew that the suffering and death of Jesus led to the Resurrection and new life. She knew how our own suffering and death brings us to new life. She knew the rhythm of life, the ups and downs we all experience. Because she knew this she survived all the little deaths, and even the worst of days did not kill her. She even emerged from her darkest days, in some mysterious way, a more alive and better person. The flower lady had learned that when she trusted, there was no such thing as "no light at the end of the tunnel." She wore her troubles well.

Easter asks us to wear our troubles well too. God is love. God cares so much that he knows the number of hairs on our heads. God turns our present sufferings to our good. God makes even our most deadly times occasions of new life. As Paul wrote, "For those who love God, everything works together for their good." God got through to the flower lady. God wants to get through to us as well.

Easter is a day of joy. It shows us the triumph of life over death, of good over evil, and joy over sorrow. Let us wear our troubles well. When someone says to you today, "You certainly look happy," you can answer, "Why not? Everything is beautiful." That's what Easter really means.

📖 The Second Sunday of Easter
(Acts 4:32-35; 1 Jn 5:1-6; Jn 20:19-31)

Easter is so big and so important that our Church gives us fifty days of Easter season to reflect on it. Why is Easter so important? It is because Easter is the keystone of our faith. Take Easter away and the whole thing comes tumbling down. Paul certainly understood this, "If Christ has not been raised your faith is empty. Your faith is worthless. You are still in your sins, and those who have fallen asleep are the deadest of the dead." That's how big Easter is.

Starting today and for the next two weeks we will reflect on what faith is, on what we believe about Jesus, and on what we believe about ourselves. Today's gospel shows us what faith is. Jesus appeared to his disciples but Thomas was not there. The other disciples said to Thomas, "We have seen the Lord." How did Thomas react? "Unless I see the mark of the nails in his hands and put my finger into the nail marks, and put my hand into his side, I will not believe."

Let's not fault Thomas for his lack of faith. Look at it this way. If we knew someone named John Doe and we knew when and how he died, and we have been to his grave, and someone told us, "We have seen John Doe." How would we react? We would say, "What are you talking about? Do you take me for a fool?" We would react just like Thomas.

But Thomas got the proof he was looking for when Jesus came back a week later. After giving Thomas proof that it was him, Jesus said to him, "Do not be unbelieving, but believe." And now we get to the crucial point. Jesus said to him, "Have you come to believe because you have seen me?" Jesus is saying, "You don't have to believe now Thomas because you have seen for yourself. Blessed are those who have not seen and have believed."

That is the heart of faith. To have faith is to believe in something we have not seen, cannot prove, and cannot understand. We have not seen the risen Jesus. We cannot prove he was raised from the dead. We cannot understand what his new, glorified life is like. Yet, Jesus asks for our faith. Blessed are those who have not seen and have believed.

Faith and certifiable proof cannot go together. It's one or the other. As soon as we are sure of something, we no longer have to believe it's true. If I show you my birth certificate that says I was born in Keokuk, Iowa, then you no longer have to believe me when I tell you I was born in Keokuk. If we are absolutely sure Jesus is risen, then we don't have to believe it. If we are absolutely sure that there is life after death, then we don't have to believe it. If we are absolutely sure Jesus is present in the Holy Eucharist, then we don't have to believe in his real presence. But if we are supposed to be sure, why didn't Jesus give us proof of these things? Why did Jesus ask us for faith? Why did Jesus say, "Blessed are those who have not seen and have believed"?

What does this reflection of faith mean to us? It means that it's all right to wonder about things we cannot prove or understand. It is all right to have doubts. Someone wrote, "He who never doubted never half believed." Doubt does not mean we are losing our faith. It means we are actually coming to faith. If we never wonder or doubt about the fantastic things we believe, we probably are not taking our faith seriously enough.

I am reminded of the woman who sent an old black and white photo to a photo finishing company. In the photo a man was seated behind a cow and all that was visible of him were his feet and legs. She sent a note with the photo. It read, "This is the only photo I have of my great grandfather. Please move the cow so I can see what he looks like." Faith is about living without seeing the whole picture. The cow is still there. Blessed are those who have not seen and have believed.

📖 The Third Sunday of Easter
(Acts 3:13-15, 17-19; 1 Jn 2:1-5a; Lk 24:35-48)

Today is our second installment about our Easter faith. Today we look at what we believe about Jesus. What do we mean when we say we believe that Jesus was raised from the dead? What is it that we believe?

I want you to imagine the Resurrection of Jesus. It is early Sunday morning in the middle of the garden. There is a tomb sealed with a huge stone. You are in that tomb. What do you see? You see the dead body of a person named Jesus, wrapped in several layers of linen cloth. The wrappings are laced with oils and perfumes. The sweetness is almost overwhelming. You stand there looking at this lifeless figure.

Wait! Did you hear something? Oh, probably just your imagination. But the wrapped figure stirs a little, now a little more. Yes, there are definite signs of life under those wrappings. Then more life. Jesus sits up and breaks out of the wrappings. Jesus is not dead! Jesus has come back to life!

Is this what we believe when we say we believe in the resurrection of Jesus? No way, my friends. We are not even close.

This is not what Easter is about. What we just imagined was not resurrection but resuscitation of a dead body to resume the same life it had before. This is what happened to Lazarus. Jesus resuscitated Lazarus to continue being the same person he was, to continue the same life he had before he died. So Lazarus lived a while longer but he died again.

Easter is so much more than this. Jesus was raised to a whole new life and existence. The risen Jesus is not the same Jesus who died on the cross. The mortal Jesus has become immortal, never to die again. The risen Jesus lives a glorious, new life we can only imagine.

The gospels tell us this as best as human words can say. Why did Mary Magdalene not recognize Jesus in the garden right outside the tomb? How could two disciples walk and talk with Jesus for miles on the road to Emmaus and not know him? When Jesus appeared in their midst, why were the disciples startled and terrified and why did they think they were seeing a ghost? Jesus had to assure them that, "It is I myself." The gospels are telling us this is not the same Jesus. The glorious, new life of Jesus is so different that they don't even know who he is.

The gospels give us other hints. What more can they give us but hints? The risen Jesus is a person whom Thomas could touch. The risen Jesus asked them, "Have you anything to eat?" They gave him a piece of baked fish and he ate it in front of them. This sounds very human and real. Yet, the risen Jesus was not bound by space or time. Jesus walked through closed doors. He simply appeared where he wanted to appear. The risen Jesus is immortal which means he experiences no aging or deterioration of any kind. These are little glimpses of glorious, new life beyond our imagination. This is what Jesus asks us to believe without seeing or understanding. This is the faith of Easter, the faith all our other faith rests on.

The Fourth Sunday of Easter
(Acts 4:8-12; 1 Jn 3:1-2; Jn 10:11-18)

Today is our final look at our Easter faith. We have looked at faith itself. We have looked at what we believe about the risen Jesus. Today we look at what we believe about ourselves.

A rabbi once said to me, "You Christians are asked to believe a lot more than we are." And he went on to say, "When you talk about your futures, you are asked to believe a whole lot more."

Scripture is filled with references to our future. God's word is written in human words and human words are totally inadequate. They can only give us glimpses and hints. And scripture is filled with hints about you and me. Let's look at three references from out of hundreds.

In the Book of Revelations we read, "Never again shall they know hunger and thirst. Nor shall the sun or its heat beat down on them. God will wipe every tear from their eyes." Think about this. What does it say about us?

In 1 John we read, "What we shall later be has not yet come to light. We know that when it comes to light, we shall be like

God." Do we hear that? We shall be like God? What does that mean?

Paul gives us our third hint when he speaks directly to how much we ourselves will be like the risen Jesus. "Christ will give a new form to this lowly body of ours and remake it according to the pattern of his glorified body." What does that mean?

It means everything we believe about the risen Jesus will be true of us, everything. The mortal Jesus has become immortal, never to die again. We shall be immortal, which means we shall experience no aging or deterioration of any kind, never to die again. The glorified Jesus was not bound by space or time. We shall not be bound by space or time. What does this mean? Do we have any idea?

Let's look at how some thinkers have tried to get a glimpse of timelessness. We live in time. All we know is time. The sun rises and sets. We move through the calendar day by day. We look at our watches to see what time it is. Time is all we know. But Jesus said, "I will give you eternal life." We cannot grasp the real meaning of eternity but here's one way to get just a glimpse.

Time is defined as a succession of moments, one following the other. This future moment becomes present, and then slips into the past. If we could take hold of the next future moment and when it becomes present, hold it there, no longer future, never to slip into the past, it would be forever now. Eternity is forever now. Isn't this mind-boggling? Remember, we are talking about ourselves and our future. If it takes a lot of faith to believe in the resurrection of Jesus to new life, then it takes enormous faith to believe this about ourselves. Oh yes! We Christians are asked to believe a lot. No wonder we are called Easter people.

Our words today are so inadequate. For years as I was ministering to people in their last days and hours, I would ask them, "When you get there, if you can, will you come back and tell me what it's all about?" No one has come back. Only recently did it dawn on me why. They could not tell me anything. There are no words to describe eternal life. There is no way I could understand.

We could draw many conclusions from this reflection on our future. I will suggest only a few. Is it possible to believe in our own resurrection to glorious new life and not have it influence our life now? Is it possible to believe in our future and have a low image of ourselves? Is it possible to believe in the resurrection of the person next to you and disdain that person in any way? And perhaps the most important, we could never do anything to deserve the future that will be ours. Is it possible ever again to doubt the enormous love God has for you and me, and his desire to have us with him forever?

The Fifth Sunday of Easter
(Acts 9:26-31; 1 Jn 3:18-24; Jn 15:1-8)

In today's gospel Jesus said, "I am the vine, you are the branches. Whoever remains in me and I in him will bear much fruit because without me you can do nothing." What a powerful image. The vine is the source of life, health, and growth of the branches. United with the vine, the branch is full of possibilities. Apart from the vine, the branch is dead. So apart from Jesus, we can do nothing.

That's a lesson we need to remember. Sometimes we feel like we're doing a pretty good job getting all our ducks in order, and becoming strong people from our own efforts. Forget it. There are no John Wayne's, no self-made people in the spiritual life. Without Jesus we can do nothing.

But as important as it is to remember our complete dependence on Jesus, today I want to emphasize something equally important. Every coin has two sides. If one side has the inscription, "Without me you can do nothing," the other side reads, "With me you can do anything." I emphasize that today because we get discouraged with ourselves. We dig ourselves into habits and ruts too difficult to get rid of. Sometimes we are tempted to let go of our idealism and big dreams because it all seems beyond us. Sometimes we feel like settling for life and for things the way they are because to pursue more just seems beyond our energy and ability.

Today Jesus is saying, "Come on. With me you can do anything. You can make a difference. You can act beyond your usual capacity. You can be bigger than you think you are. This is true because it is not just you; it is you and I together. Know this and go and bear much fruit."

What is the fruit Jesus wants from us? "I give you one commandment; love one another as I have loved you." With Jesus, our vine, we are enabled to love beyond our natural inclination. Naturally we are inclined to love those who love us. We are inclined to measure our love to protect ourselves. We are inclined to love those who deserve our love. But Jesus says, "With me you can do anything." You can love the spouse maybe you are tired of loving. You can love him or her more than you have. We can love the person who does not like us. We can love the unattractive person.

A little girl was showing her dolls to her grandmother. Her grandmother asked her, "Which one do you like the most?" The little girl said, "You promise that you won't laugh if I tell you?" Her grandmother promised. Then the little girl picked up the most miserable looking doll of all. "Why do you like that one the most?" her grandmother asked. She said, "Because it needs my love more than the pretty ones do."

The difference between us and the real spiritual heroes and saints is that they knew they were in union with Jesus and they lived beyond their normal capacity. Let's hold on to our idealism. Let's keep our dreams. Let's not say that anything about us is impossible. Why? Because Jesus is the vine, we are the branches, and with Jesus we can do anything.

The Sixth Sunday of Easter
(Acts 10:25-26, 34-35, 44-48; 1 Jn 4:7-10; Jn 15:9-17)

Today's gospel is from the 15th chapter of John. It is part of Jesus' last discourse with his disciples. It is Holy Thursday night. When he is finished they will go to the Garden of Gethsemane to pray. Jesus will be arrested. There is no time to mince words, no time to question, challenge, or debate; no time to analyze or look for hidden meanings. The last discourse is it. Every word counts. What are Jesus' last words?

"This is my commandment; love one another as I love you. No one has greater love than this, to lay down one's life for one's friends. This I command you, love one another." This is straight forward, direct, and clear. So we got it, right? Did we? Then why have we analyzed and parsed these words of Jesus for 2,000 years? Why have countless books and seminars tried to explain to us what Jesus meant and did not mean? Why have they tried to tell us how to love and how not to love? After 2,000 years of this I think Jesus would say, "Stop it. Just do it."

If we get it, then why do some in our church say that our Church has gone soft with all this emphasis on love? Why do they say that we need to get back to some basic and hard realities like discipline and obedience? Why do they say that we need to emphasize more the tough stuff, the rules and regulations because religion is not supposed to be just easy, warm and fuzzy stuff about love?

Anyone who has really loved knows that love is not soft, warm, and easy. Anyone who has really loved would say to God, "Please, Lord, ask me to obey all the rules and regulations. I can do that. But please don't ask me to really love people. That is tough."

Remember the final words of Jesus, "This is my commandment, love one another as I love you. No one has greater love than this, to lay down one's life for one's friends." Do we think this was warm and fuzzy for Jesus? How disciplined and obedient was Jesus to actually do this? He showed us just how tough love can be. In fact, I think Jesus made an essential connection between love and death. He loved us so much that he died and in dying brought new life to us.

Whenever you and I really love, we too die to some part of ourselves to bring life to others. We see it all the time: a son or daughter patiently caring for the elderly parent who does not even know who they are because of Alzheimer's disease; the single mom or dad working two jobs to give a more decent life to the kids; mom or dad up all night caring for the sick child; the teenager risking the loss of some "so-called" friends by befriending the classmate nobody likes. Think about it. Look around. We are surrounded by people who are dying to something in themselves to bring life to others. They don't bother to analyze what they are doing, they just do it.

St. Paul understood what Jesus meant. "If I speak with human tongues and angelic as well, but do not love, I am a noisy gong." If I started speaking like the angels I would think that I was someone special. "If I have faith great enough to move mountains, but have not love, I am nothing." If I had faith strong enough to move mountains, I would think I was pretty holy. "If I give everything I have to feed the poor and hand over my body to be burned, but have not love, I gain nothing." Oh, wait a minute. If I gave everything I have to the poor, if I was ready to give up my life to be martyred, I would guess I had become holy in heroic ways. But without love, we gain nothing from anything we do. Paul knew what Jesus meant. Do we?

The Seventh Sunday of Easter
(Acts 1:15-17, 20a, 20c-26; 1 Jn 4:11-16; Jn 17:11b-19)

Our scripture readings today cause me a problem because they do not inspire me. And that is a problem because I stand here ready to speak to you about them. And if they don't inspire thoughts and feelings in me, if they don't stir up my juices, then what am I supposed to say to you?

Look at our first reading from the Acts of the Apostles. It tells us how they chose a successor to Judas who betrayed the Lord. What can I say? I'm glad they chose a successor to Judas?

Look at our second reading. John is writing more about love. John writes beautifully about love, but I talked about love last week and John is saying pretty much the same thing again today.

Look at our gospel. It's part of Jesus' prayer for his disciples after the last supper. It's beautiful, if somewhat vague. I could talk about how Jesus uses the term "world" in different ways. In this reading Jesus makes the world seem evil. Yet, at other times we read things like, "God so loved the world he sent his only Son to save it." But I don't want to talk about that. It really doesn't make my adrenalin flow.

But wait. Let's go back to that second reading by John. It's all about love, but there is one sentence that is sort of leaping up at me from the page. There is one sentence that makes me want to react. John writes, "We have come to know and to believe in the love God has for us."

Now wait a minute, John, speak for yourself. Maybe you have come to know and to believe in the love God has for you, but I think you are pretty presumptuous to speak for us. How can you say "we" have come to know and believe in the love God has for us? Do you think we have? Have you really come to know and to believe in the love God has for you? Have I?

Look at us. Look at our flaws and imperfection. Look beneath our human imperfection to our downright smallness and pettiness which makes us so hurtful sometimes. Look at our downright foolishness and sinfulness, our selfishness, greed, lust, and dishonesty. Now let's ask that question again. Have you really come to know and to believe in the love God has for you, for you, the person you are? Have I come to believe in the love God has for me, the person I am?

That's why I want to say to John, "Wait a minute, John. Speak for yourself, but don't presume to speak for us folks." After all, if we really knew and believed in God's love for us, why do we question God so much? Why are we always saying, "Why did God will this?" Or, "How can God treat me this way?" Or, "If God is so good, how can he let this happen?"

What we are really saying is, "If I were God, if I was all-knowing and all-powerful, I would do a better job than he's doing." Or, as Woody Allen said in the movie, "Love and Death," after he died and went to heaven, "Yes, there is a God. It's just that he's an underachiever."

So if we really have come to know and to believe in the love God has for us, then why do we think we would love more and care more if we were God? Speak for yourself, John. After all, if we really knew and believed in God's love for us why would we fear him so much? Why would we be afraid of his judgment? Why would we feel like he's keeping score on us? Why would we feel so guilty? Why would we kick ourselves around so much over our foolishness and sinfulness? If we really knew and believed that God loves us, why aren't we happier people? Why aren't we ecstatically happy people? Why aren't we more optimistic, more encouraged, and more alive?

Speak for yourself, John. But what I really want to say is, "Lord, let John speak for us too. You have told us every way you can that you love us just as we are. What more can you do than offer your only Son to prove your love for us? What more can you say?"

Lord, make us the people John is speaking for. With John, let us say gladly, "We have come to know and to believe in the love God has for us."

📖 Pentecost
(Acts 2:1-11; 1 Cor 12:3b-7, 12-13; Jn 20:19-23)

It is Pentecost, the feast of the Holy Spirit. The Holy Spirit is sometimes referred to as the forgotten person of the Holy Trinity. Sometimes we think of the Holy Spirit as kind of quiet and passive, operating behind the scene. Nothing could be further from the truth. The Holy Spirit is God at his most active and powerful level.

In our first reading the Holy Spirit is a strong, driving wind, a fire, and a bold proclamation. When the disciples received the Holy Spirit on Pentecost they were changed forever. They were changed from the fearful people locked in a room to people who proclaimed Jesus to the ends of the world, and, at the cost of their own lives. No, there is nothing bland about the Holy Spirit. Only the Spirit can touch our hearts and change our lives so deeply that we become different people. We are talking about power beyond our wildest dreams.

The Holy Spirit is not past history. Pentecost is not a feast for us to marvel at what happened then. Jesus promised this same Holy Spirit to us. Could he state it any more convincingly than he did in Luke 11? "What father among you would hand his son a snake when he asks for a fish? Or hand him a scorpion when he asks for an egg? If you, then, who are sinful, know how to give good gifts to your children, how much more will the Father in heaven give the Holy Spirit to those who ask him?" So, if we ask we are guaranteed a response. But before we ask, I propose two questions we really need to think about.

First, what do we expect from the Holy Spirit? My guess is that we expect little from the Holy Spirit. We would be surprised if the Spirit did anything dramatic in us. Maybe we are used to living with low expectations. Maybe we have been disappointed when we had high expectations of someone and they were not met. Maybe we protect ourselves by keeping our expectations low so we will not be disappointed again. Do we think the Holy Spirit will disappoint us if we expect too much? The Holy Spirit of driving wind and fire and boldness will not only meet our expectations, the Spirit will vastly surpass our expectations. Let us raise our expectations. Let us be prepared to be surprised. If the Spirit is anything, the Spirit is surprise.

Our second question is, do we really want to be surprised? If you are like me, I prefer all surprises to be planned and on my schedule. But of course that is no surprise at all. Do we really want to be changed or would we rather leave well enough alone? We all carve out our comfort zones. We set those lines and boundaries within which we feel comfortable. When we step beyond our boundaries we experience fear and discomfort. We can choose to live the rest of our lives within our comfort zone or we can accept God's invitation and ask for the Holy Spirit. Sure, the Holy Spirit will surprise us, stretch us, and make us our full, free selves. But this second question is crucial. The action of the Holy Spirit within us hangs on this because God respects our choices.

Do we want the Holy Spirit? How much the Father wants to give the Holy Spirit to those who ask him. Why not ask, knowing that we are asking for surprises and trusting that God wants only the best for us.

📖 Trinity Sunday
(Dt 4:32-34; Rom 8:14-17; Mt 28:16-20)

Today we celebrate the greatest, most central mystery of our faith – the blessed Trinity.

When I was younger and, I thought, smarter, I used to try to explain certain mysteries of our faith with philosophy and theology. Now that I am older and, hopefully wiser, I don't do that anymore. I simply stand in wonder and awe before something far beyond my understanding.

If there is ever a day to stand in wonder and awe it is today. The only reason we know there is a Trinity, which means that there are three persons in God, is that God thought enough of us to reveal to us just a glimpse of God's own inner life. It is impossible to be a Christian and not believe in the Trinity because the whole New Testament is filled with references to God, the Father, the Son, and the Holy Spirit. So God gave us a glimpse and we stand in wonder and awe before this glimpse of divine inner life.

I will give you one theologian's thoughts on the mystery of the Trinity, but as I do I will try not to repeat the true story about a four-year-old boy who was sitting in the front row and was getting restless as the priest kept talking about this wonderful mystery. The boy got more restless as the priest talked on and on. Finally the priest said, "I don't know what else I can say to explain this to you." The four-year-old answered loudly, "Then say amen and sit down."

The theologian I cite is St. Augustine. He wrote that he did not find the language of Father, Son, and Holy Spirit the best terminology to teach about the Trinity. His best language speaks of God as Lover, Beloved, and the Love between them. From all eternity God is Lover who gives himself away perfectly to the Son. The Son accepts being loved and returns it perfectly. And the Love, the perfect bond of mutual self-giving is the Holy Spirit. This explosion of love beyond our imagination is the heart of everything that exists. Since God is love itself, wherever we find self-giving love, we find God.

Think about that. God is the love we find in our own hearts. God is the love between husband and wife, and between parents and their children. God is the love we have for one another, and the love we show to the stranger and the least among us.

The ancient hymn "Ubi Caritas Et Amor, Deus Ibi Est," says it well, "Wherever there is charity and love, there is God.

This reminds me of my own true story about a young boy in the first row on Trinity Sunday. I was trying to say something about it and I asked, "What does it mean to say that God is our Father?" The little boy's hand went up immediately, and he said, "If God is our Father that means we are brothers and sisters." Out of the mouth of babes…

We have not solved the mystery of the Trinity today, and we never will. But maybe these words have given us something to ponder; something we can take home that can make a practical difference in our lives.

God is not out there somewhere. God is everywhere. God is right here. God is in every one of our loving thoughts, words, and deeds. God, you are really awesome!

📖 Body and Blood of Christ
(Ex 24:3-8; Heb 9:11-15; Mk 14:12-16, 22-26)

Today we celebrate Jesus' gift of himself to us in the Holy Eucharist, an almost unbelievable gift.

When Jesus first announced that he would give his flesh as food and his blood as drink, it sounded so outrageous that most of his followers left him. But Jesus did not recant. He turned to his closest disciples and asked, "Will you too leave?" They answered, surely without understanding the depth of what Jesus said, "Lord, to whom shall we go? You have the words of eternal life."

On Holy Thursday night Jesus did what he promised. He took bread, said the blessing, and said, "Take it. This is my body." He took the cup, gave thanks, and said, "This is my blood." We Catholics believe the substances of bread and wine are changed into the substances of the body and blood of Jesus. What words could Jesus have used to state more powerfully, "Yes, this bread and wine is really me"? "I become present to you. I actually become part of you when you receive me in the Holy Eucharist."

It is a gift beyond our imagination. It is a gift that we need to think about so we do not become overly familiar with it. This is a basic weakness of our human nature: not to stay impressed with something we become too familiar with. The gift of the Holy Eucharist deserves our thought and reflection.

Something else deserves our reflection today and that is what we have done with the gift of the Holy Eucharist throughout our history. Jesus gave himself to us as pure gift. We have moved from that to making the Holy Eucharist a gift limited only to those who see themselves as worthy to receive it. What absolute heresy it is for anyone to judge himself or herself as worthy of Jesus. What heresy for anyone to judge another person as unworthy of Jesus. I cannot believe this thinking has made Jesus happy. Jesus said, "I came for sinners, not the righteous." It seems to me that it is more inappropriate for a righteous person to approach the Holy Eucharist because he felt he deserved it than for a sinner to approach it because he needed Jesus.

Let's look at our unworthiness. Right before we receive the Holy Eucharist we say, "Lord, I am not worthy to receive you." Do we mean this? I hope to God we do. You are not worthy. I am not worthy. We will never be worthy of Jesus. Worthiness means that we have done something that entitles us to the Holy Eucharist. The Holy Eucharist becomes a reward for being good. Jesus gave himself to us because he knew we needed him to be good. "Come to me all of you who labor and are burdened, and I will refresh you."

See how we have turned it around? I cannot believe Jesus is happy about this. I feel sad when I meet people who have stayed away from the Holy Eucharist because someone told them they are not worthy. I was asked by a family I had never met before if I would do a Catholic burial service for their 86-year-old mother. She had been a very active Catholic until she was divorced thirty years ago. Someone told her she was no longer welcome at church, no longer worthy of the Holy Eucharist. She lived her last thirty years without the gift of Jesus in the Holy Eucharist. Her children told me what a good, loving woman she was. Would I bury her? You know the answer to that. What made my heart heavy was that I did not know her thirty years ago so that I could have told her that Jesus still wanted her.

Don't let that happen to you. Don't let that happen to anyone you know. If there is anyone here or anyone you know who is staying away from the Holy Eucharist for whatever reason, invite them to talk with me. I will open all the doors I can to invite them back to the Holy Eucharist. I believe Jesus is happy when we do this.

📖 Birth of John the Baptist
(Is 49:1-6; Acts 13:22-26; Lk 1:57-66, 80)
(When June 24 is on Sunday)

Today we celebrate the birth of John the Baptist. Look at the events surrounding his birth. Zechariah and his wife Elizabeth were advanced in years. Elizabeth was sterile. Then Zechariah received a message from on high. Luke says the message came from the angel Gabriel, "Your wife Elizabeth shall bear a son whom you shall name John." Zechariah responded, "How am I to know this? I am an old man and my wife too is advanced in age." Then the angel replied, "You will be mute, unable to speak, until these things take place because you have not trusted my words."

Imagine how their relatives and neighbors handled this situation. "Dear old Elizabeth with child? And what happened to Zechariah? He can't speak." Which brings us to today's gospel. Elizabeth's neighbors and relatives knew the Lord had shown his great mercy to her by enabling her to give birth at her age. Then Zechariah could speak again. Then fear came on all the neighbors and they discussed these matters throughout the country of Judea. They were saying, "What then, will this child be?" Can we see this picture?

These people huddled on dusty roads, around village wells, and synagogues talking about these events. They kept asking, "What will this child be?"

When you were born, were people amazed at the circumstances of your birth? Were they shaking their heads in wonder as they looked at you in your bassinette? Were they gathering at water coolers and supermarket aisles asking about you, "What shall this child be?" Probably not. But we are still like John the Baptist in one way. God had a plan for John and people had great expectations of him. God also has a plan for us and people have expectations of us, maybe not as great as John's, but still expectations.

God wanted John to be the forerunner of Jesus. God wanted John to announce the arrival of Jesus and give witness to him. The people expected more of John. He had a large following, probably larger than Jesus and people expected him to be the Messiah.

Luke tells us that, "The people were full of anticipation, wondering in their hearts whether John might be the Messiah." John tells us, "Jewish priests came to ask John, "Who are you?" His response was, "I am not the Messiah. I am the voice crying out; make straight the way of the Lord. One much greater is coming after me." As John caught sight of Jesus, he exclaimed, "Look, there is the Lamb of God!"

Yes, there were great expectations of John from his birth. But John knew who he was. He was true to who he was. He did not meet all those expectations. He was true to God's plan for him. What about us? God has a plan for us. God calls us to respond wholeheartedly to Jesus. He calls us to be his disciples in our world today. He calls us to have our faith be the light of the world, and to show our little part of the world the love, mercy, and graciousness of our God.

But people have all kinds of expectations of us. When we were little, most of our expectations came from our parents. As we grew up we were pressured most by the expectations of our peers. We were told to fit in, join in, and to be like everybody else. We were told to conform and not run the risk of being excluded. As grownups we are surrounded by expectations. When I was ordained I thought every priest was expected to drink scotch and play golf. Well, I met only one of those, and I don't play golf.

What are some of those expectations that people and society have of us? They still want us to fit in, and to be like everybody else. Society will allow some room to be different, but not too different. When we are too different we challenge other people and their values. We are saying by our lifestyle that we do not go along with things the way they are. We do not fit in with a society that values wealth, beauty, and youth.

We don't fit in with a society that preaches "me, my satisfaction, and my pleasure before the needs of others." Wholehearted people scare society.

How do we meet the expectations of others? How important is it to us to be approved by our society? Do we ever feel the loneliness of being different? The answers to these questions might indicate whether we, like John the Baptist, know who we are, and whether we are true to God's plan for us.

THE FEAST OF SAINTS PETER AND PAUL
(Acts 12:1-11; 2 Tm 4:6-8, 17-18; Mt 16:13-19)
(When June 29th is on Sunday)

Today is the Feast of Saints Peter and Paul. Peter and Paul are true saints, but they are not angels. Sometimes we get saints and angels mixed up. Angels are pure spirits. They do everything right. Saints are human beings. They are flesh and blood as well as spirit. Human beings don't do everything right. We sin, make bad judgments and choices, but we can still be saints. Scan the New Testament and see what kind of people appeal to Jesus the most.

Zacheus, the chief tax collector, was a really big crook. With equal enthusiasm he welcomed Jesus into his home and responded to Jesus' call to change his life, to be a saint.

Mary Magdalene was a woman who had seven devils cast out of her. She, who was close to Jesus and was the first person the risen Jesus appeared to.

The apostles James and John, whom Jesus called "The Sons of Thunder," immediately left everything to follow Jesus, but they wanted to be first. Their ambition was to sit to the right and left of Jesus when he came to power. This disturbed the other apostles.

Simon, also known as the Zealot, breathed fire at the Romans who occupied his country and wanted to expel them violently.

No angels there, but all were saints. Now let's look at the two saints we honor today.

Peter can be described as loudmouthed, spontaneous, enthusiastic, and big-hearted. He was spontaneous to the point of being impulsive. When Jesus asked Peter to follow him, Peter did it spontaneously, leaving everything behind him. When Peter saw Jesus walking on the water, he spontaneously stepped out of the boat into the water and took a few steps before he thought, "Oh my God, what am I doing out here?" and began to sink. Peter was enthusiastic. He was a man of strong feeling who often spoke before he thought. When Jesus told his disciples that he would have to suffer and die, Peter took him aside and protested, "No, this should not happen to you." Jesus reprimanded him, "Get out of my sight. You are not judging by God's standards." When Peter told Jesus, "Though everyone else may have their faith in you shaken, mine will never be shaken," Jesus said to him, "I give you my word, Peter, before the cock crows tonight you will deny me three times." A few hours later, Peter cursed and shouted to a servant girl, "I do not even know that man." Peter carried his spontaneity and enthusiasm to the end.

Tradition tells us that he died by crucifixion, but Peter asked to be crucified upside down because he was not worthy to die as Jesus did. Peter was not an angel, but he was a saint.

Now look at Paul. Paul can be described as a driven, dynamic, feisty, and stubborn man. Acts tell us that Paul was a Pharisee breathing murderous threats against the Christians. When Ananias was told to instruct Paul, he was scared. He asked, "Why me? I have heard from many sources about this man." Paul fought with his coworkers. Barnabas wanted John Mark to join them. Paul refused saying that, since he did not join them on another mission, he was not fit to travel with them. Barnabas and Paul fought so bitterly that Barnabas could no longer travel with Paul. All of these men are saints, none were angels. Paul was a driven man. He did not know when to shut up. Acts tell us he talked on and on past midnight and a certain young lad named Eutychus, who was sitting at the window, went to sleep and fell out. At Philippi, a girl was following Paul around and shouting, "These men are servants of the most high God!" She did this several days until Paul got annoyed with her and told her in the name of Jesus Christ to get lost. Paul took his passion and enthusiasm to Rome where he died by the sword for the Lord. An angel, no, but a true saint.

What can we draw from these people whom Jesus chose to be

especially close to him? The stuff of which great sinners are made is the same stuff which makes great saints. Isn't it wonderful what Jesus can do with people like Peter and Paul, and with people like us? Angels, no, but we are all called to be saints.

The Twelfth Sunday of the Year
(Job 38:1, 8-11; 2 Cor 5:14-17; Mk 4:35-41)

We have probably heard this gospel hundreds of times, but does it strike us as curious or strange? Let's look at it again to appreciate what's really happening in this gospel.

Let's look at the scene. Jesus wanted to cross the sea, so off they went. A violent squall came up. Oh boy! That's bad news. A squall is sudden and violent wind that creates real danger in the water. The boat was already filling up with water. That's what's happening.

Let's look at those disciples. They were seasoned men of the sea. They were professional fishermen and knew the weather well. They could tell the difference between false alarms and real trouble and they knew they were in real trouble and about to capsize and sink with their boat.

Let's look at the disciples' reaction to this danger. They must have wondered how Jesus could sleep through all this. They woke Jesus and said to him, "Don't you care that we are perishing?" Wouldn't we have reacted in the same way, and probably a lot sooner than the disciples did?

Now comes the strange part of our gospel. We look at how Jesus responded. He said, "Quiet. Be still." The wind ceased and there was a great calm. Then Jesus said, "Why are you terrified?" That's a strange question. Why are they terrified? Why wouldn't they be terrified?

Then Jesus asks an even stranger question, "Do you not yet have faith?" What are you saying to your disciples, Jesus, and to us? Are you saying that when we feel like we're drowning in the unfairness and problems of life that we are to believe in you so strongly, and trust you so completely that we will not be overcome with fear and will not throw in the towel? Yes! Jesus is asking for complete confidence and trust in him no matter how tough things seem to be. Is Jesus asking too much of us? We may feel that way but I think our own experience tells us he is not asking too much.

I'll bet that after some years those disciples could look back on that dangerous time and say, "Yes, we should have trusted." I'll bet we can look back at some tough times, times that could have done us in, but did not, and see now how God was with us. I can look back at a time in my life that was very dark. I could not see any light at the end of the tunnel for some months. It was a time of pure faith. I was just going through the motions and hanging on by my fingernails. But finally, I did see the light and emerged from the darkness a stronger and better person. That which could have done me in God actually made a time of grace and growth for me. We all have experiences like this.

Sometimes we need to rise above the details of our lives and see the bigger picture, and the bigger picture is remarkable. Can we say miraculous? The only reason we are here today, and the only reason we are the people we are today is that the Lord has brought us through everything to this day. So when we feel out of control like the disciples in the boat, Jesus is asking us to believe and trust that our God loves us, and is present to us always, especially when we need him most.

The Thirteenth Sunday of the Year
(Wis 1:13-15, 2:23-24; 2 Cor 8:7-9, 13-15; Mk 5:21-24, 35b-43)

Last week was about faith and trust in God's love and care no matter how tough life seems to be.

Remember last week when the big storm came up on the sea and the disciples were terrified with good reason? Jesus said to them, "Why are you so terrified? Don't you have faith?" Well I guess Jesus really wants us to get this message because we have more today. Today Jairus pleaded with Jesus to save his twelve-year-old daughter, "My daughter is at the point of death," and Jairus, like any parent, was full of fear and anxiety. Then the report came, "Your daughter has died." Jesus said to Jairus, "Do not be afraid, just have faith."

What in the world was Jesus asking of his disciples and Jairus when he asked them for faith? The word "faith" comes from the Latin *fides,* which means trust. It is defined as unwavering belief and trust in God. We saw that last week and we see it again today: trust is what Jesus asked of them and is asking of us.

Our basic question today is, "How are we living our day-today lives? Are we basically fearful people or are we people who believe and trust in God's love and care for us? If fear dominates our lives, we are constantly saying things like, "I'm afraid of this…maybe this will happen to me…What will I do if…?" We live as though the next thing around the corner is going to get us. If faith and trust dominate our lives, we say things like, "My God, look what I have survived to get to this day. Hey, I have not only survived, I have come out of tough times a lot better person for them. It's true, for those who love God; everything works together for our good. Thank you, Lord, for taking good care of me."

Are we basically fearful people or people of faith and trust? The most common form of fear is worry. Some years ago I told you about a doctor who studied his patients to see why they worried so much. I'll tell you again because we need to be reminded of this. Here's what the doctor found:

- *Forty percent of his patients' worries were about things that never happened.*
- *Thirty percent worried about matters which were entirely beyond their control.*
- *Twelve percent of their worries were related to the physical ills which were caused or aggravated by worry itself.*
- *Ten percent of their worries were about friends or relatives who were quite able to look after themselves.*

- *Eight percent of their worries were about matters that really needed their attention. But even in these cases worry was not the remedy.*

Could you and I be one of his patients? Is this the way we are living?

Jesus did not promise us a worry-free life. He did not say that we will never have reason to be concerned. But Jesus did say, "Don't worry so much. Don't be anxious about so many things. Why? It is because we have a God who cares a lot about us and who knows even the number of hairs on our heads. We have a God who loves us more than we can imagine and Jesus is asking to trust that love and care.

We can look at it this way: every tomorrow comes with two handles. We can take hold of tomorrow with the handle of fear or the handle of trust. How will we take hold of tomorrow?

📖 The Fourteenth Sunday of the Year
(Ez 2:2-5; 2 Cor 12:7-10; Mk 6:1-6)

In our gospel today Jesus returns to his hometown of Nazareth. Jesus grew up there and spent most of his life there. It was not a big town. He had family there and knew the people. So when the Sabbath came he began to teach in the synagogue and many who heard him were astonished. Now to be astonished means to be really put back on your heels. Why were they astonished? Why were they reeling on their heels?

At first glance it would seem they knew Jesus too well to take him seriously. But I think there is more to it than that. In fact, they took him so seriously that they were astonished. "Where did this man get all this?" Get all what? "What kind of wisdom has been given him?" What did Jesus teach that was so different from the others? "Is this not the carpenter, the son of Mary? Don't we know his whole family?" And they dismissed him and, in fact, took offense at him.

But let's get back to why they were astonished. "Where did he get all this?" Get all what? "What kind of wisdom has been given him?" What was he teaching that was so different? It was not only what he taught, but how he taught.

Throughout the gospels we are told that Jesus "taught with authority, and not as their teachers of the law." Other rabbis would simply quote well-known teachers and then offer their own commentary. Not Jesus! He taught with authority, "You have heard it said…, but now I say to you." When Jesus spoke, he clearly meant to be the final word on the subject. This might be why they were astonished. What he taught might be the reason they took offense at him.

What did Jesus teach? Now I am going to tread on thin ice. I am going to try to summarize the whole message of Jesus in two lines. This is thin ice because there is always more to the gospels than meets the eye. But I will do it because I think it can be helpful to simplify the gospels by seeing through the details to the heart of the matter. Here are my two lines. Jesus taught how much God loves us. Jesus calls us to respond to God's love with our whole hearts.

Jesus taught how much God loves us. Yes, God loves us more than the best parents love their children. God loves us unconditionally, no matter what we have done. God loves us so much that he sent his own son to be for us. God loves us so much that he has adopted us as his own children and made us heirs of eternal life with God.

This was perhaps astonishing news to Jesus' contemporaries who viewed God in a more impersonal way. To them God was the "great power" way up there somewhere. This is perhaps astonishing news to us who still find it difficult to believe God could possibly love us that way.

Jesus calls us to respond to God's love with our whole hearts. With authority, Jesus teaches that nothing less will do. He does not want half-hearted, lukewarm people. Jesus does not want good people who say their prayers faithfully or good people who obey the letter of the commandments and go to sleep feeling justified. Jesus wants our very best. He wants our whole hearts. That's it. Maybe an over-simplification, but that's how I see the whole message of Jesus. Believe you are so loved by God and respond in like manner.

Perhaps this astonished Jesus' contemporaries who were schooled in strict observance of the letter of the law. Law asks for a minimum response. Jesus asks for the maximum. Perhaps this is astonishing to us who are so inclined to settle for good rather than best; to us who don't like being stretched beyond our neat and tidy comfort zones. Is it possible that we too might take offense at Jesus? Is he asking too much?

Let us be astonished. Let us open our eyes to the wonderful possibilities still within us. If we believe that God loves us in this way, anything is possible. There is no such thing as too much.

The Fifteenth Sunday of the Year
(Am 7:12-15; Eph 1:3-14; Mk 6:7-13)

I'll bet today's gospel is one of those we consider an event of past history. Jesus sent out his disciples two by two to proclaim the good news he had taught them. This gospel is full of words like "unclean spirits," "walking sticks," and "tunics," which reflect a culture of past history. So we are inclined to say, "That's nice, but what does today's gospel have to do with me?" It has everything to do with us, especially those three powerful words: "summoned," "sent," and "went."

Jesus wanted his good news proclaimed to the ends of the earth. How could this happen? Jesus spoke to limited audiences for only three years. He never traveled more than one hundred miles from his birthplace. So he sent his disciples forth and they made other disciples who went forth to the ends of the earth. This has been happening right up to our present day.

You and I have the faith today. Where did we get it? Not from Jesus or the apostles. They have not spoken a word for nearly two thousand years. From whom did our faith come? It came from ordinary people like you and me. It came from parents, teachers, friends, and neighbors, all ordinary people, but all disciples proclaiming the good news to us. And now it is our turn. We are the disciples of Jesus today.

Now for that first powerful word, "summoned." To be summoned implies greater urgency than just being asked. Yes, Jesus summons us. The second powerful word is "send." Jesus sends us forth. I know our immediate reaction to such powerful words is, "Who me? Jesus summons me? Jesus sends me forth? Oh come on, there are a lot of people better suited than I am to do that." Our hesitation is just like the prophet Amos in our first reading. "I was no prophet. I was a shepherd and dresser of sycamores." Amos said to the Lord, "Who me?" And the Lord said to Amos, "Go." We are just like the prophet Jeremiah. He said to the Lord, "Who me? You are making a mistake, Lord. I am too young and do not speak well." The Lord said to Jeremiah, "Go."

Today the Lord summons you and sends you forth. Our mission is not to drive out demons and cure the sick. Our mission is not to stand at a street corner shouting that Jesus has saved the world. Our mission is not to go door by door telling people how much God loves them. This sounds like Mission Impossible. Our mission is to go forth to our families, workplaces, and neighborhoods and to reflect the good news of Jesus by what we say and by who we are. We do it as ordinary people in ordinary ways. This is Mission Possible, and we are doing it.

Many of the people who come to see me about their spiritual lives do not come because they know me. They come because you have sent them. Almost every week I meet a new person here, not because they know me, but because you invited them. This brings us to our last powerful word. The disciples "went off." We conclude each Mass sending you forth. We say," Go in peace to love and serve the Lord." Let that be a constant reminder that we are disciples who are summoned and sent forth.

The Sixteenth Sunday of the Year
(Jer 23:1-6; Eph 2:13-16; Mk 6:30-34)

Today's gospel could be subtitled "Life gets tedious, doesn't it?" So this gospel comes right in the middle of a hot summer. This is the time of the year that school is out and the kids are home, and our patience and stamina are more easily tested. Today's gospel is for all of us who know what we mean when we ask, "Life gets tedious, doesn't it?"

Webster's Dictionary describes it pretty well. It says that "Tedium," which comes from the Latin *Taedium,* means a time of weariness and strained anxiety. First, we will look at Jesus who in this gospel is having a very tedious day. Then we will look at our own lives when we are having tedious days.

In Mark's gospel Jesus and his disciples had been preaching and tending to the needs of people to the point of exhaustion. People were coming and going in great numbers and the disciples had no opportunity even to eat. They couldn't even take a lunch break. So Jesus said to them, "Come away by yourselves to a deserted place and rest a while." So the disciples went off in the boat to a deserted place.

Oh what relief! Finally, Jesus and the disciples were alone as they drifted quietly across the sea. They could take a breath and unwind without all those people tugging at them for more. They really needed a break. But look at what those demanding people did. They saw the disciples leaving in the boat and figured out where they were headed. They even told people from other towns so they could join them, and they all hastened to arrive at the place before the boat landed.

That's the scene in our gospel. Can we imagine how Jesus and the disciples felt as their boat approached their deserted place? Now they saw an even bigger crowd of people waiting for them to tug on them some more. Now let us apply this scene to our own lives. I'll bet there are many mothers here who have had days you would not choose to live over. Have you had those exhausting days that frazzle your nerves? Have you had days when the kids were noisy and out of sorts and never stopped tugging at you for one thing or another? What about days when the air conditioning fails and the car won't start? "Please, Lord, I can't give anymore. Give me a break. I need a deserted place to rest a while."

And you, dads, you have the same kind of days. There are those days when everyone at work is edgy, including your boss. There are those days when you have a nagging headache and you make mistakes that you usually don't make. What about those days when you are on the way home and get stuck for three traffic lights because it seems the drivers ahead of you are more concerned with their cell phones than with moving? Then, there are those days when you walk into your house and the air conditioning is not working and you say, "Don't anyone talk to me. Just pour me a drink." We single folks have tedious days too.

This is what our gospel is all about. How did Jesus react? When he saw the crowds of people, did he throw up his arms and say, "Enough is enough. Can't you wait until tomorrow? Turn the boat around. We'll park in the middle of the sea if we have to." How did Jesus react? When Jesus saw the vast crowd, his heart was moved with pity and he continued to teach them many more things.

Now you may react, "That's great, but that was Jesus. I am not Jesus." That is true. But since we have days like Jesus, our gospel is encouraging us to hang in there. Our gospel is not asking us to overwork. We need rest, quiet, and peace. Jesus knew this and wanted to give it to his disciples the same as he wants us to have it. Our gospel is about giving a little more when we have already given enough. Our gospel is about how Jesus loved so much that he found the inner resources to give more when he had given enough. Our gospel is saying that we can do the same thing. We have the inner resources to be even heroic when we are called to be. But we do not do it by ourselves. I believe that Jesus is especially close to us when life gets tedious and, with Jesus, we can do it. Since we know that we are acting beyond our ordinary capacity, even in the midst of all the tedium, we can take a deep breath and say, "Thank you, Lord. Without you I can do nothing. But look what I can do with you."

The Seventeenth Sunday of the Year
(2 Kgs 4:42-44; Eph 4:1-6; Jn 6:1-15)

Our gospel today speaks to all of us who face problems that look too big for us to deal with, and to all of us who feel overwhelmed by a situation. What does it feel like to be overwhelmed? It feels like stuff is coming at us from all sides; like everything is catching up with us; like it's all too much to deal with; and like we are about to drown in something over which we have no control. It's a tough feeling and I think it hits us all from time to time.

Our gospel today is about being overwhelmed by a situation too big to cope with. A large crowd followed Jesus out into the desert. There were five thousand men. What about the women and children? Our gospel shows some of the sexism that was prevalent in those days. Commentators say counting the women and children could make the crowd as large as twenty thousand people.

So here are twenty thousand hungry people and there is not a McDonald's or a supermarket in sight. Jesus surveyed the whole impossible scene, and then he turned to Phillip and asked him, "What can we do about this? Where can we buy enough food for them to eat?" Phillip said that even two hundred days' wages of worth of food would not be enough for each of them to have a little. Phillip was overwhelmed. He felt powerless. Then Andrew said that there was a boy who had five barley loaves and two fish, but wondered what good these would be for so many people. Andrew was overwhelmed. What he had was too small to cope with this.

The point of the gospel is that Jesus did not take the problem away from his disciples. He did not say, "Don't worry about this. I'll take care of it." Instead, Jesus turned to his disciples to see what their available resources were. He wanted to know what solutions they could bring to the problem. He wanted to see what he and his disciples could do together.

This raises a question. What do we do when we are faced with problems that seem too much for us? We can worry and fret by ourselves until we feel overwhelmed enough to admit, "I can't handle this by myself." We can step away from the problem and turn it all over to God to solve. Sometimes this is called "letting go and letting God." But our gospel is telling us that neither one of these is the right approach. Jesus does not want us to go it alone. Jesus loves us and is concerned about us and wants to be part of the solution. Jesus does not want us to just step away and put it in the hands of God and wait for a solution. He wants us to bring our resources to the problem. As someone wrote, "We will work as if everything depended on us, and we will pray as if everything depended on God." That's the point of the gospel. Jesus wants it to be a joint effort.

We probably feel like Andrew. We've got five loaves and two fish, but what good are these? This is all that Jesus needs. "Bring your resources to me, as meager as they are, and together we'll make it happen." Every one of us has his or her five loaves. Our five loaves are our resources, talents, gifts, and energy, as meager as they may seem. That is all the Lord is asking for to do big things together.

📖 The Eighteenth Sunday of the Year
(Ex 16:2-4, 12-15; Eph 4:17, 20-24; Jn 6:24-35)

Last week we saw the huge crowd that was fed with the loaves and fish. A part of that crowd is still looking for Jesus. Jesus said to them, "You are looking for me because you ate the loaves and were filled." They said to him, "What can we do to accomplish the works of God?" Jesus answered, "This is the work of God, that you believe in the one he sent."

Throughout the gospels Jesus is consistent in asking us for one thing, faith. So today let's examine our faith. On a faith scale from 1 to 10, (10 being the strongest faith and 1 being the weakest faith), where do you measure your faith? Well no matter where you measure your faith, you are a 10. We are all 10s on the faith scale. I will tell you why.

Faith steps in when we do not have certitude. If I know something is true without any possibility that I am wrong, then I have certitude. I do not need faith. If I know something is true beyond the shadow of a doubt, I have certitude. I do not need faith.

How many of us believe in God? Is there anyone of us who

can prove beyond the shadow of a doubt that there is a God? We can't, and yet we believe. Can you see what faith you have? How many of us believe that the Bible is the word of God? Can anyone of us prove that the Bible is the word of God? This is an act of great faith in the Church which teaches us that the Bible is the word of God. How many of us believe that Jesus Christ is the Son of God and that he is divine? This is a great act of faith in the writers of the gospels who tell us Jesus is divine. How many of us believe there is life after death and that we are destined to live forever? None of us knows for sure what happens at death and beyond death. Is it any wonder that I say we are all 10s on the faith scale? My friends, it is almost unbelievable what we believe.

Today's gospel brings us to even more faith. Jesus said, "God's bread comes down from heaven and gives life to the world. I am the bread of life." Do we hear Jesus? Can we believe this? Can we believe that every time we receive the Eucharistic bread we receive Jesus because Jesus himself is the bread of life? We just broke through 10 on the faith scale.

The older I get the more I wonder about faith. I find our faith something to wonder about and the more I wonder the more wonderful faith becomes. What a gift to be able to believe. Today I invite you to wonder with me. I hope you have your doubts. Yes, you heard me correctly. Many times people have said to me, "I have doubts. I think I am losing my faith." Well I believe the opposite is true. To doubt means we have faith. When we ponder all that we believe, how can we erase any trace of doubt from all this? To doubt means that we are wrestling with our faith, and the more we wrestle, the stronger we become.

As you approach the Holy Eucharist today, be aware that you are making a great act of faith. Every time we approach Eucharist, may it be a reminder of the great gift we have; and may it be yet another time to pray, "Lord, I believe. Help my unbelief. Thank you for my faith, Lord."

The Nineteenth Sunday of the Year
(1 Kgs 19:4-8; Eph 4:30, 5:2; Jn 6:41-51)

The people murmured because Jesus said, "I am the bread that came down from heaven." Now, if we had been in that original audience, how would we have reacted? Do you think that we would say, "Oh, stop that murmuring"? Hardly. We would have joined the crowd questioning just who does Jesus think he is. "Is that not Jesus, the son of Joseph? Do we not know his father and mother? Then, how can he say, 'I have come down from heaven?'"

I have a theory that it is easier for us to believe Jesus now than if we had lived in his time. We have the advantage of knowing how he ended his life, and of knowing about his resurrection to new life. We have the advantage of two thousand years of tradition and teaching to throw some light on Jesus and his meaning.

Back to our gospel. Jesus said, "Stop murmuring. Amen I say to you, whoever believes has eternal life. I am the living bread that came down from heaven. Whoever eats this bread will live forever. And the bread that I will give is my flesh for the life of the world." No wonder most of his followers said,

"This is too much. We can't take that." And they left him. But Jesus did not back down at all. He did not say, "Oh please, try to understand. I am speaking in a metaphorical way." No, Jesus became even more specific. "The bread that I will give is my flesh. This bread is really me. When you eat this bread I become truly present to you. You and I become one."

Still, Jesus' presence in the Holy Eucharist is a mystery, which means that we cannot prove it. We have to believe it. "Amen, I say to you, whoever believes has eternal life." And we do believe. That's why we are here again to celebrate this mystery. But very easily we become creatures of habit. We can get used to the most extraordinary things.

Someone wrote, "If familiarity does not breed contempt, it takes off the edge of admiration." That, I think, is a danger for all of us. As a priest, I celebrate up to ten Masses a week, so I need to reflect on what I'm doing. I remember visiting a church and seeing a plaque in the vesting sacristy, it read: "Celebrate this Mass as if it were the last one of your life." I don't want to lose that edge of admiration. And there is a danger for Eucharistic ministers. They need to stop and think about what they are doing. You are offering to others this bread that has come down from heaven and the cup of salvation. You don't want to lose this edge of admiration. And all of us who receive the Holy Eucharist need to stop and think. "I am about to receive Jesus himself who promises eternal life to me because I receive him in faith." We don't want to lose that edge of admiration.

Does receiving the Holy Eucharist frequently make any real difference in our lives? Sometimes we think, "I seem to be the same old person. I don't seem to change or get better." We may not be able to point to specifics every time we receive the Holy Eucharist. But I know my potential for selfishness and sinfulness. I don't want to imagine myself without this presence of Jesus in the Holy Eucharist. How about you?

We are the most blessed and privileged people in the world. Let's think about it so we will not lose that edge of admiration. Then one day, when faith turns into vision, we will see that Jesus meant every word he said.

📖 Twentieth Sunday of the Year
(Prv 9:1-6; Eph 5:15-20; Jn 6:51-58)

We continue from last week with the sixth chapter of John's gospel about the Holy Eucharist. Please read this chapter. It is nothing less than shocking. It shocked those who heard it from Jesus himself. It still shocks some people today. Whenever I am asked, "How can you Catholics believe you receive the body and blood of Christ at communion?" I simply say, "Don't take my word for it. Read John 6 and tell me what you think."

In today's gospel Jesus said, "The bread I will give you is my flesh." The Jews quarreled over this saying, "How can this man give us his flesh to eat?" Did Jesus back off? Did he say, "I didn't really mean that"? No. He said, "Amen, amen I say to you. Unless you eat my flesh and drink my blood you do not have life. My flesh is true food and my blood is true drink."

When I was a young priest I was assigned the "inquiry class," which was a series of lessons for those who expressed some interest in becoming Catholics. I felt somewhat confident when we came to the subject of the Holy Eucharist. I filled the blackboard with the philosophy of Aristotle and the theology of St. Thomas Aquinas that I had learned so well in the seminary. I talked about substance and accidents (appearances). I reminded people that at the wedding reception at Cana Jesus changed both the substance and appearances of water into wine. At Mass the priest, following Jesus' command to do this in his memory, changes the substances of bread and wine into the substances of his body and blood while the appearances remain the same. By the time I got to the end of the blackboard I felt pretty good about the whole thing. Had I made good sense out of the Holy Eucharist? Had I explained this great mystery to their satisfaction? No way. Forget it. No one can explain the mystery of the Holy Eucharist. It is totally beyond our grasp. Now that I am older and hopefully wiser, I simply stand in awe of this mystery and pray, "I believe, Lord, help my unbelief."

When Cardinal Timothy Manning was auxiliary bishop of Los Angeles he hosted a dinner for some well known theologians. He sat quietly as they debated the intricacies of our language about the Holy Eucharist. Finally Cardinal Manning interjected, "I just wish I had the faith in the Holy Eucharist that my mother in Ireland has."

You know what I think the bigger mystery is? Why in the world would Jesus do such a thing? Why would he want to give himself to us under the appearances of bread and wine?

Why would he want to become part of us just as all food and drink actually become part of us and nourish us? There is only one answer, love. Jesus loves us so much that he wants to become literally one with us. Such love is beyond our grasp. It's another call to faith, to believe that it is true.

📖 THE TWENTY-FIRST SUNDAY OF THE YEAR
(Josh 24:1-2a, 15-17, 18b; Eph 5:21-32; Jn 6:60-69)

For the past two weeks we have looked at Jesus in the sixth chapter of John's gospel. He is promising the gift of himself in the Holy Eucharist. "I am the living bread. Whoever eats this bread will live forever. And the bread that I will give is my flesh for the life of the world."

We saw that Jesus' audience murmured about this. They quarreled among themselves saying, "How can this man give us his flesh to eat?" Can we fault them? What would we have thought if we were part of that audience?

Today we deal with the final part of John's sixth chapter. What was the final result of Jesus' shocking revelation about his gift of himself in the Holy Eucharist? Many of Jesus' disciples said, "This is a hard saying; who can accept it?" Jesus said, "Does this shock you? The words I have spoken to you are spirit and life. But there are some of you who do not believe."

What was the final result? "As a result of this, many of disciples returned to their former ways of life and no longer accompanied him." It was back to the fishing boats or other pursuits for them. They thought they had found someone special in Jesus. They found that he was too much for them.

This must have saddened Jesus, but it did not surprise him. He must have seen this result. But he did not back down. He was even willing to lose his closest disciples and friends if they could not believe him. Jesus turned to the twelve, "Do you also want to leave?" Simon Peter answered him, "Master, to whom shall we go? You have the words of eternal life. We have come to believe."

Thank God for Peter and the twelve. Thank God for their gift of faith. Their faith led to the reality of the Holy Eucharist during the Passover supper that Holy Thursday night. Luke describes the scene in chapter twenty two, "Then, taking bread and giving thanks, he broke it and gave it to them saying, 'This is my body to be given for you.'" He did the same with the cup, saying, "This cup is the new covenant in my blood which will be shed for you. Do this as a remembrance of me."

Thank God for the gift of faith given to the apostles. Thank God for the gift of faith given to us. With that gift you and I are able to echo the words of Simon Peter, "You have the words of eternal life. We have come to believe."

What is the real final result? Every minute of every day and night somewhere in the world Mass is being celebrated. Every minute a priest is repeating Jesus' words over bread and wine, doing this as a remembrance of him. When Jesus promised to be with us until the end of time, he really meant it. In the Holy Eucharist he is with us. He becomes a part of us. This leads to his other promise, "Amen, amen I say to you, whoever believes has eternal life. Whoever eats this bread will live forever." Such faith, such love.

The Twenty-Second Sunday of the Year
(Dt 4:1-2, 6-8; Jas 1:17-18, 21b-22, 27;
Mk 7:1-8, 14-15, 21-23)

Heart makes all the difference in the world. We know when a football or basketball team is just going through the motions. Come on! Put some heart into it! A choir or orchestra leader will not settle for everyone just getting the right notes. Come on! Put some heart into it!

Today Jesus says, "This people honor me with their lips but their hearts are far from me. In vain do they worship me." Jesus says, "Come on! Put some heart into it!"

The Pharisees honored God with their lips. They recited the prescribed prayers meticulously. They carefully followed all their customs and traditions. They washed their hands, cups, jugs, and kettles. They did everything right and Jesus said, "You cling to human tradition but disregard God's commandment to love God and others with your whole hearts." Come on! Put some heart into it.

Now let's move from the Pharisees of two thousand years ago to ourselves today. God is not satisfied with our prayer, ritual, or observances of laws and regulations if our hearts are not into it. God wants your heart and mine.

Let's apply this to three areas. First, let us apply it to prayer. It is easy for us to go through the motions of prayer without our hearts in it. We may have certain prayers that we say every day. We say novenas, rosaries, or grace at meals, but it is so easy to just say them. We may say them dutifully each day, then close our books, put away our rosaries and say, "That's over now," like we have just finished a tedious chore. Yes! It is quite possible for us to honor God with our lips, but our hearts are far from him.

Let's apply this to Mass and to other ritual prayers. Here too we can fall into just going through the motions. We can be here and make all the proper responses and we can do all the externals with our hearts somewhere else. We may be thinking, "I hope this is a short Mass because I would really rather be about something else. Let's get Mass out of the way so we can get on with our day. "In vain they worship me."

Let's apply it to the commandments and our religious rules and regulations. How easy it is to obey the letter of the law and to do everything legally correct. How easy to go to bed, make a quick check of the commandments, "No, I did not break any of them today," and go to sleep feeling justified. It is possible to observe all the commandments and to go through all the motions correctly and not even be Christian!

Why? It is because God wants much more than external observances. God wants our hearts. Jesus said, "Hear me, all of you, and understand. It is not the outside or external that counts. It is the inside, the heart that matters."

So today we need a heart check. We need a check today to see if we have heart trouble. Our heart check will be with words. What words describe us when we are involved in something with our whole hearts? What words describe us when we are not? When we are about something whole-heartedly, what words come to mind? What about "exciting, challenging, joyful, and passionate"? What about "dull, routine, unexciting, joyless"? Okay, our heart check is simply this, which set of words best describes our religious lives? We need to take the test. We need to know because Jesus says, "Put your heart into it."

📖 The Twenty-Third Sunday of the Year
(Is 35:4-7a; Jas 2:1-5; Mk 7:31-37)

In Mark's gospel today Jesus is the fulfillment of Old Testament prophecy. The first reading of Isaiah says, "Here is your God. He comes to save you. Then will the ears of the deaf be cleared." But you might say, "Wait a minute. What does this have to do with me? My hearing is perfect." Or you may say, "I may have some problem hearing, but I am not deaf." But I believe that our gospel today speaks to much more than physical deafness. We do not hear one another in so many ways. We often hear that anguished question, "Why can't you hear me?" Are we going through life deaf to so much around us? Are we deaf even to those closest to us?

One reason for our deafness is our prejudice. But again you might say, "Wait a minute! You're not talking about me. I am not a prejudiced person." None of us want to think we are, but we need to look at the possibility. Prejudice comes from the Latin word which means to "pre-judge." To pre-judge means that we have our minds made up about someone or some group of people. When we have our minds made up we are prejudiced toward that person or group. We may be prejudiced in favor of or against them, but either way we are prejudiced. Here are a few examples.

Do we have our minds made up about young people? "You know, kids today have no sense of responsibility, and they have no values. We can't trust them or depend on them. I wasn't that way when I was growing up. What's happening to this younger generation?"

It works the other way too. Do we have our minds made up about the older generation? "You know, my parents are too old to understand me; they are hopelessly stuck in their ways. There is no sense talking to them. They can't hear me."

Our deafness from prejudice can apply to any group we have our minds made up about. "Poor people on welfare are simply lazy. They are just looking for a free ride. If they had any character they would get to work and take care of themselves." When I'm in line at the supermarket and a person ahead of me uses food stamps, do I think, "Why should they get free food when I pay for mine? If they worked as hard as I do, they could pay their own way too." We can also be prejudiced toward other groups such as homosexuals. "If they really wanted to they could straighten themselves out." Or we may be prejudiced about political groups like Republicans, Democrats, liberals or conservatives. My God! We have our minds so made up we can hardly speak to one another. We are living in a seriously divided country.

Our deafness can be most devastating to those closest to us. Often in counseling couples I ask if they are hearing what each other is saying. When I ask one to repeat what the other just said, there are surprising results. I find that they have heard the opposite of what was said. They hear what they want to hear or what they expect to hear. How often our prejudgment, mindset, and expectations cause that anguished cry, "Why can't you hear me?"

Jesus came to heal us of our deafness to one another. Jesus wants to put his fingers into our ears and pray, "Be opened." If we still think that today's gospel does not apply to us, I ask you to do one brave thing today. Ask your spouse or child or parent or special friend to give you an honest answer to one question: "Do I really hear you?" When we get our answer, then maybe we too will beg Jesus to lay his hands on us.

📖 Triumph of the Cross
(Num 21:4b-9; Phil 2:6-11; Jn 3:13-17)
(When September 14 is on Sunday)

Today is the Feast of the Triumph of the Cross. What in the world are we celebrating? If someone says to you, "You are my cross in life," do you feel triumphant and positively affirmed? How can we associate these two words "triumph" and "cross"? There is no way the disciples of Jesus could associate crucifixion with triumph. They were completely opposite, contradictory words.

Let's look at the history of the cross. The Romans borrowed crucifixion from the Persians. They used it as capital punishment for slaves and non Romans. Because no matter what crime a Roman citizen committed, he was never low enough to be crucified. Peter and Paul both committed the same offense. They preached a new religion about Jesus. Peter was crucified. Paul was not because he was a Roman citizen.

The cross was reserved for the low-life scum of the earth. Ancient Roman art shows a crucified person with the head of a donkey. To be crucified was the ultimate shame, disgrace, and failure, yet, today we celebrate the triumph of the cross.

No wonder Paul wrote in 1 Corinthians 1, "We preach Christ crucified, a stumbling block to Jews and an absurdity to Gentiles. So where is the triumph? Paul continues, "The message of the cross is complete absurdity to those who are headed for ruin. But to us who are saved, it is the power of God."

As Jesus said in our gospel, "Just as Moses lifted up the serpent in the desert, so must the Son of Man be lifted up, so that everyone who believes in him may have eternal life." God does work in strange ways. God turned failure into success, death into eternal life. So today we celebrate this paradox, the Triumph of the Cross.

The contradiction of the cross continues in our own lives. Jesus said to you and me, "If you want to come after me, you must take up your cross each day and follow in my steps." The cross has come to signify trial and suffering, and suffering of one kind or other is a part of all our lives. I'll bet you that every single one of us is dealing with some kind of suffering or anxiety right now. And you are too smart to cover that bet because we all know it is true. But God works in strange ways in our lives too. We live with the contradiction of the cross.

Quite naturally, we all want to avoid suffering, but what we want to avoid we cannot. When our suffering becomes intense, it should destroy us, but it does not. In fact, and here is the paradox, when we embrace our suffering in faith, it actually deepens us and enlarges us as persons. If we could erase all the suffering from our lives up to this minute, we would be very different people here today. We would be much less than we are. What an apparent contradiction. What an apparent absurdity.

I am reminded of the words of Helen Keller. Imagine the suffering of living in darkness through our whole lives. Helen Keller fought this cross in anger and frustration for years. Yet, she came to say what certainly appears to be an absurdity, "I thank God for my blindness." What? "Yes, I thank God for my blindness because through it I have found my God and myself."

Today's feast remains an absurdity and stumbling block to everyone who does not believe. But for those of us who do believe, we celebrate today the Triumph of the Cross in the life of Jesus and the Triumph of the Cross in our own lives.

The Twenty-Fourth Sunday of the Year
(Is 50:5-9a; Jas 7:14-18; Mk 8:27-35)

Today's gospel has one of the most familiar lines in the New Testament, "Whoever wishes to come after me must deny himself, take up his cross and follow me." We have heard that very often from the time we were kids. Today's homily is about the mystery of suffering in our lives. You know what? We are not going to solve this mystery today, but we must speak to it. Why?

Because today's homily is addressed to all of us who have some cross in our lives. How many of us would that be? All of us.

Today's homily is for all of us who ask, "Why, why must the cross always be there? Lord, why is this happening to me? Lord, it just seems like one thing after another. Lord, why are you doing this to me if you love me so much?" That's why we must speak to it today, so we can answer two questions. Does God want us to suffer? What is the difference between suffering and taking up our cross?

Does God want us to suffer? We answer this with another

question. Do you want someone you love to suffer? Absolutely not. God is love. God loves us with total and unconditional love. God cannot want us to suffer for the sake of suffering. We need to be clear about this. Have we ever said to a suffering person, "This is God's will"? Never say that. Jesus said, "Whoever wishes to follow me must take up his cross." Does this mean that we suffer more because we follow Jesus? No. Do Christians suffer more than non-believers? No. When a baby is baptized, does God say, "Oh boy! Now we've got another one we will make suffer"? Absolutely not. All of this thinking is opposed to a loving God who does not will suffering to a loved one anymore than we do.

What is the difference between suffering and taking up one's cross? As we said, suffering is part of everyone's life, which includes people of faith and no faith. But because we have faith and because we do follow Jesus, our suffering can be embraced as a cross which makes all the difference. Look at the difference. Suffering itself is resisted or, at best, tolerated. But as strongly as we naturally try to avoid suffering, when it comes, we can in faith embrace it or, at least, accept it as a cross.

Suffering itself can lead to bitterness, cynicism, and despair. A cross can lead to inner peace, hope, and wholeness. Why? It is because God in his love can bring good out of evil. God can make us better persons because of our cross. In our hearts we know this is true. If we could erase all the suffering from our lives we would not be half the people we are today. That's the mysterious difference between just plain suffering and taking up our cross.

Jesus certainly knew what he was talking about. He lived this mystery of suffering. Why did he have to suffer so and die to save us? I can't answer that but our faith tells us that by his cross he saved the world. Our gospel today is inviting us to take up our own crosses in faith and to follow in the footsteps of Jesus. We are not walking alone. We are following him who walked the road before us and who walks with us every step of our way.

📖 The Twenty-Fifth Sunday of the Year
(Wis 2:12, 17-20; Jas 3:16, 4:3; Mk 9:30-37)

I think today is a test to see how you and I handle a gospel that is counter-cultural, a gospel that goes against everything our society treasures.

Jesus asked his disciples, "What are you arguing about?" They remained silent because they had been discussing who was the greatest. They were too embarrassed to answer. Those disciples were just like us. Isn't it encouraging to know that they, all of whom became saints, had all the human weaknesses and flaws that we have? We all have a need to be seen as important. It's part of our human nature.

What does Jesus tell his disciples? "If anyone wishes to be first, he shall be the last of all and the servant of all." Next time you go to lunch tell the waitress, "You are number one. You rank first among us." What will she say? Probably nothing because she will not want to offend you. But when she gets to the kitchen she'll say, "Wow! I've got a real dingy at table two." Tell that to the person who bags your groceries.

You'll probably get a weak "Thank you," and a befuddled look. Catch the garbage man. He'll probably look at you and ask what you've been smoking.

Why is this so? Because the gospel is so counter to our American culture. It does not fit our society. Our culture preaches the opposite, "Be first. Be number one." Our culture preaches competition. It values winners and has little time for losers.

Look at business. Who wants to be number two? We hear in a rental car commercial that number two is working harder. Why? To become number one, of course. In athletics we see the same thing. Every time there is a game there is a winner and a loser, but who wants to be the loser. Our lifestyle mirrors the same theme. We max out our credit limits in order to keep up with the Joneses, or at least appear to keep up so people won't think we are inferior. This competition and the need to be recognized as important are in the very air we breathe.

Now we come to our gospel. "If anyone wishes to be first, he shall be the last of all and the servant of all." What does this gospel mean? Does God want all of us to be waitresses, grocery baggers, and garbage men? No. We all must serve and receive the service of others. Does God want us to hold back and use only half of our talent and energy so we will not excel, not get to the top? No. God has gifted us and wants us to use our gifts and become the best people we can be.

I think the key to our gospel is found not in things around us but inside us. What kind of people are we? What are the values which motivate and drive us? Are we living the values of our culture or the values of Jesus? Are we driven by competitive values that smile on winners and disdain losers? Are we driven by the values of Jesus: true humility, unselfishness, and giving ourselves in service to others?

True humility is simply the basic truth of who we are. We acknowledge that we are nothing and have nothing that does not ultimately come from God. We know in our hearts what Jesus meant when he said, "Without me you can do nothing." And in truth we accept our strengths and successes along with our weaknesses and failures, and we say, "Thank you, Lord, for gifting me."

We are people who take seriously the call of the gospel to serve the needs of others. We put who we are and what we have into that service. We want to become the best we can be. We want to fully utilize our talents and strengths and not bury them. And when we become our best, we will not be concerned about how society ranks us. We will rank first in God's eyes because, in truth, we will see ourselves as the last of all and the servants of all.

📖 The Twenty-Sixth Sunday of the Year
(Nm 11:25-29; Jas 5:1-6; Mk 9:38-43, 45, 47-48)

Good morning class. Yes, this is catechism class and it's time for a quiz. But don't get nervous. There are no wrong answers to this quiz. So whatever you answer I won't make you sit in the corner. But I do want you to think about your answer before you respond. Our question is about the existence of hell. Are you ready?

Do you believe in hell, a place of unending punishment? Do you not believe in hell? Are you not sure what you believe about hell? Because I am not sure, please do not call me a heretic. Even Pope John Paul II writes that he has difficulty merging eternal punishment with God's mercy and God's will that everyone be saved.

Is our Church going soft on this question? Was John Paul II getting confused over such an important matter as hell? Some people think so. They say, "That's the trouble with our Church today, it is confusing things. We need to get back to the days when we had definite answers. We had lists of mortal sins and if you commit one and die you are going to hell. We need to bring back those powerful parish mission preachers who used to scare the hell out of us."

But our Church has not grown soft. We have simply become more humble in our answers. Humility is truth. In all truth we do not have definite, provable answers about afterlife, heaven, or hell. But that does not mean that we do not believe in afterlife with its rewards and punishments.

Whenever we speak about heaven and hell we must speak in images. Dante's Inferno gives us a powerful image of hell. Mark's gospel today gives us another image of punishment. But as John Paul II cautioned us, these are only images. In today's gospel Jesus is not speaking of hell but of Gehenna. Everyone who heard Jesus knew about Gehenna. It was the garbage dump for the city of Jerusalem. It was always smoky with smoldering fires. Worms and all kinds of vermin crawled through the garbage. So Jesus said, "It is better for you to enter life maimed than with both hands go to Gehenna with its unquenchable fire. It is better to enter the kingdom of God with one eye than with two eyes be thrown into Gehenna where the worm does not die." This is powerful imagery and Gehenna has become one of our images of hell.

Is there a clear message in today's gospel? You bet there is. What is it? Without a doubt Jesus is talking about the reality of sin, the true evil of sin. Do we need to be convinced of this? Just look around us and see the human suffering and unspeakable evil that comes from sinful choices. Just look within us and see the suffering we have brought on ourselves and others by our sinful choices. Sin is real and we will not get confused about that.

Without a doubt God's word in the Old Testament and the New Testament speaks of reward and punishment. It does make a difference how we live. We are responsible for our choices and decisions. Our lives are worthy of reward or punishment. But we don't want to live out of hope for reward or fear of punishment. Oh, that's okay if fear is the only thing that will keep us from sin, but God does not want us to live that way. For example, little Johnnie has really messed up his room. His mom tells him to clean it up. Johnnie says, "I will if you give me a dollar." His dad tells him to clean up his room or he will be punished. Johnnie says, "Okay, Dad, I'll do it because I don't want to be punished." This attitude leaves mom and dad cold. Why couldn't Johnnie do it because he loved them?

If we live out of hope for reward or fear of punishment, I think it leaves God cold. Why can't we respond out of love? If we have any idea of the enormity of God's love for us, how can we not respond out of love?

The Twenty-Seventh Sunday of the Year
(Gn 2:18-24; Heb 2:9-11; Mk 10:2-16)

We have another tough gospel today. This one is about marriage and divorce. A priest asked me what I was going to say about it. He said he would choose one of the other readings to talk about. But as tough as it sounds, we have to deal with it. Otherwise, we miss the power of what Jesus is saying.

Scripture scholars tell us they think Jesus' words are an absolute prohibition against divorce and re-marriage. This is the scriptural basis for our Church's stand on the permanence of marriage. Our Church teaches that when two people are validly married, they are married until death. So, if Jesus taught an absolute prohibition against divorce and remarriage, then it seems the case is closed. There's nothing more to say. But this is too simplistic.

Jesus is talking about people who are really married. Our Church is talking about people who are validly married. What does this mean? It means that when two people get married their consent is true and total. They are promising fidelity for life. They are promising to take the good times and the bad times together. Their true and total consent is verified by their behavior after getting married.

Sometimes behavior after marriage shows clearly that consent to fidelity and permanence was really not there. A young man who was married only a few months went to his priest and said he wanted a divorce. He said that any relationship in need of work was not worth staying in. I don't know what planet he came from, but on this planet there is no such thing as a marriage that does not take work. When behavior after marriage shows that true consent was lacking, that's when our Church offers a declaration of nullity which permits them to marry again.

Let's look at the heart of the matter. Today Jesus teaches the permanence of marriage and that ideal remains every time two people get married. Ideally they will stay married for life. Why is permanence so essential to the institution of marriage? Marriage is the most intimate and sacred relationship possible to human beings. It is so special that scripture uses marriage as the image of Jesus' bonding to the Church. Marriage is the deepest expression of love and the source of life itself. It is a relationship which by its nature demands permanence and fidelity, which asks for your very best. You are asked to work at it as hard as you work at your Christian life because your marriage is your way to eternal life. That is the truth of Jesus' teaching today.

But what about the millions of Catholics in the United States who are divorced and re-married? Is there no room for them in our Church? Have they committed the unforgivable sin? No. We are all sinners and God forgives all our sins. That's why the Vatican Sacred Congregation of the Doctrine of Faith replied to a letter from Cardinal Medeiros of Boston, who asked, "What do I do with all these people who want to participate fully in Church?" The Sacred Congregation of the Doctrine of Faith replied by stating the ideal of permanence in marriage. We must never dismiss or water down this ideal. But then the Sacred Congregation of the Doctrine of Faith went on to instruct bishops and pastors to use every means at their disposal, including the External Forum (annulment) when possible, and the Internal Forum (forum of conscience) to reach out to these people and invite them to full participation in Church.

Why does our Church allow Internal Forum solutions to these cases? It is because our Church teaches clearly the primacy of conscience. It is the one law we must always follow. It takes precedence over other laws and no one is to be prevented from acting in accord with his or her conscience.

Our gospel today is a call to married people to give your

marriage your very best. It is also a call to divorced and remarried people to look deeply, honestly, and prayerfully into your hearts and to be true to the law of God written in your hearts.

📖 The Twenty-Eighth Sunday of the Year
(Wis 7:7-11; Heb 4:12-13; Mk 10:17-30)

In looking over past homilies I have given on this Sunday of the year, I realized that I usually talk about how the man in the gospel went away sad because he had many possessions. It was more difficult for him to make radical decisions because he had more to lose. I also have talked about why the disciples were so amazed when Jesus said how difficult it is for wealthy people to enter the kingdom of God. Jesus stated just the opposite of what was common Jewish belief and that was that wealth was a sign of God's special favor. I also have talked about what there is about wealth that makes it more difficult to enter the kingdom of God. Is it the power it gives over other people? Is it the sense of security and independence that lessens one's dependence on God? These are all common themes for today's gospel, but we can easily apply them to someone else.

But today I follow another insight and it includes all of us. The man in the gospel was a good man. He had observed all the commandments from his youth. He had reached a plateau in his spiritual life. He was doing everything right, but he sensed that there was more to it. He was right. Jesus called him to his next step of spiritual growth, to radical poverty, in order to follow Jesus with his whole heart, unfettered by things of this world. Jesus called him. He heard the call. He could not take the next step because he had too much to lose.

You and I are in this gospel too. Some of us feel that we have reached a plateau in our spiritual growth. We are living a good life and are avoiding at least the big sins. We are following all the rules. We are faithfully attending Mass, participating in the sacraments, and saying our daily prayer. Yet, like the man in the gospel, we know in our hearts that there is so much more to it than that. We know that there is a next step and we feel God nudging us to it even though we may not be sure what it is.

We know Jesus' call to the man in the gospel. What is your call? What is mine? What is our next step in spiritual growth? Most importantly, when we sense what it is, will we respond or fail to respond?

There is a fear in us about becoming too holy and about becoming too close to Jesus. We are afraid of what he may ask of us. Today's gospel does not help us. It intensifies our uneasiness because we do not want to be poor. "If I get closer to Jesus, what will it cost me? I am healthy and I don't want to lose that. I am well thought of and I want to keep my good reputation and the respect of others. What will you ask of me, Jesus?"

We act like Jesus wants us to suffer or that he wants to deprive us or bring us down in some way. Jesus is not interested in taking away anything from us or to make us suffer. Whatever he calls us to is purely for our own good. What else could he want for us since he loves us so much?

My friends, if we feel we are resting on a spiritual plateau, if we feel we are static rather than in motion, if we know there is so much more to it, and deep down want the more, then trust Jesus. That's all. Trust him. How often did he tell us, "Do not be afraid"? Listen to the nudging inside and know that it comes from someone who loved us to death.

📖 The Twenty-Ninth Sunday of the Year
(Is 53:10-11; Heb 4:14-16; Mk 10:35-45)

Mark's gospel today is almost a repeat of his gospel we heard on the 25th Sunday of the year. Perhaps you remember that the disciples were arguing among themselves who was the greatest. And Jesus said, "If anyone wishes to be first, he shall be the last of all and the servant of all."

Now the disciples are at it again. James and John came to Jesus and said, "We want you to do for us whatever we ask of you." What a presumptuous request. Give us whatever we ask for before we tell you what we want. Jesus did not bite. He asked, "What do you want me to do for you?"

They answered, "Grant that in your glory we may sit one at your right and the other at your left." And they were not thinking about glory in heaven. They were ambitious to bask in Jesus' glory as the powerful, messianic leader.

Jesus must have felt sick inside. "When will you, my closest followers, ever get my message?" The other ten disciples were no better. When they heard this they became indignant because they did not want James and John to be picked over them. I can hear Jesus heave a big sigh and say, almost in desperation, "Whoever wishes to be great among you will be your servant. Whoever wishes to be first among you will be the slave of all."

Isn't it somewhat consoling to know those disciples, yes, those future saints, were just like us? Whether we admit it or not, deep down inside we all have this need to be important, the need to be noticed in some way, the need to be respected and to count in the eyes of other people. We don't have to deny it or even apologize for it. It seems to come with the whole package of being human.

A friend asked Leonard Bernstein, the great orchestra conductor, what was the hardest instrument to play. He replied, "The second fiddle. I can always get plenty of first violinists, but to find one who plays second violin with as much enthusiasm, now that's a problem."

So what is Jesus saying to us today? Just as the Son of Man did not come to be served but to serve, he wants us to be like him. Our greatness is not in the trappings society gives to important people, titles, places of honor, certificates of appreciation, etc. We may enjoy all of these, but they do not make us important to Jesus. Our greatness is not found in power or influence, fame or fortune, popularity or prestige. We may enjoy all of this, but it does not make us important to Jesus. The only thing that makes us important to Jesus is our loving, practical service to others just as the Son of Man did not come to be served but to serve.

The Thirtieth Sunday of the Year
(Jer 31:7-9; Heb 5:1-6; Mk 10:46-52)

We have just heard the story of Bartimaeus, the blind beggar in today's gospel. Today I want to change all our names. Hi, I'm Fr. Bartimaeus Fuller. I'm happy to meet you, Bartimaeus. Why do I say that we are all Bartimaeus? It is because we are all blind. "Wait a minute, Father. I've got good eyesight. You can't call me blind." But still I do because I think we are all blind or at least we do not see as Jesus sees. Let me give you just a few examples.

We do not see human needs around us. There are many in our midst that live below the federal poverty level. Ask the people at St. Vincent de Paul about the endless needs with which they deal every day. Ask those who help with our winter shelter program about our homeless guests. We do not see the needs of our loved ones around us. We get so filled up with our own needs that we don't see the needs of others. We're all too busy with our own agendas. We have all had the experience of expressing our need and nobody hears us. That's a really bad feeling. Doesn't anyone care?

We do not see God as Jesus sees God. We still doubt that God loves us unconditionally no matter what we do. We still doubt that God has completely forgiven us, so we continue to carry our baggage of guilt. We see a different God than Jesus sees.

We do not see ourselves as Jesus sees us. We do not see that we are so precious to God that God knows each one of us by name. God knows even the number of hairs on our heads. We do not see that we are so important to God that Jesus died to save us. St. Thomas Aquinas said that if you were the only person to be saved, Jesus would die just for you. We see ourselves as much less than Jesus sees us.

Hello Bartimaeus. Call me Bartimaeus too. Like Bartimaeus, you and I need to cry out, "Lord, I want to see. I want to see things as you see them. I want to judge and value things as you judge and value them. I want what is important to you to be important to me. I want your priorities to be my priorities. Lord, what it all means is, I want to see as you see."

Do we really or are we afraid of such vision? Would we rather just stay the way we are because to see as Jesus sees might be more of an eye-opening experience than we care for? We had better think and pray about this before we ask for it. God, who wants only the best for us, just might give it to us.

Jesus asks you and me today, "What do you want me to do

for you?" If we say, "Lord, I want to see," Jesus will say, "Your faith has healed you," and WOW! We will see our God, our world around us, the people around us, and ourselves in a whole new way.

The Thirty-First Sunday of the Year
(Dt 6:2-6; Heb 7:23-28; Mk 12:28b-34)

How many of us feel insecure in some way? Oh, come on, don't we all feel insecure? It seems to be a part of our human nature. We can feel insecure about our health, finances, relationships, and all kinds of things. And this naturally flows into our spiritual lives and becomes even more intense because now we are dealing with the mysterious unknown. We are talking about our eternal salvation and, if there is anything we want to feel secure about, that's it. So look what we have done through the centuries to mask our insecurity.

Our Church has over 2,000 canon laws telling us how to live within safe boundaries. We have developed a huge number of approaches to prayer and spirituality. Let's see, shall I follow the Ignatian way, the Benedictine way, the Franciscan way, or the way of Divine Mercy of Sister Faustina? And there are many more from which to choose.

To overcome our insecurity we have devised all kinds of guarantees and assurances that we are saved: make the nine first Fridays and you are guaranteed heaven; wear the scapular and you will not die without a priest; and we have countless novenas, indulgences and prayer forms that will do the trick. And none of this comes from the Gospel. All this is fictitious because no one can offer us such guarantees. If you have an eternal life insurance policy signed by the Pope himself, don't believe it. There is only one guarantee from Jesus which we shall see in a few moments.

In the name of our security see what we have done to complicate our religious lives. We have made it heavy and confusing, especially to young people. We feel the weight and confusion ourselves and sometimes don't we just want to cry out, "Lord, just tell me what you want me to do and I will do it! Just tell me clearly!"

I hear Jesus answering that plea, "How many times do I have to tell you? How many times before you get the message?" He tells us again in today's gospel in answer to the question, "Which is the first of all commandments?" Again Jesus tells us, "Love God with your whole heart. Love your neighbor as yourself." So why do we resist Jesus' principles of loving God and each other? Loving God and neighbor is too general. In our insecurity we want more explicit direction from God. We say, "Tell me what to do in this case and that one. Give me a how-to-manual to answer my doubts."

Bill Cosby had a funny routine in which he played Noah in the process of building the ark. At one point Noah becomes exasperated with all the ridicule he's getting for building this monstrous boat on dry land and with all the problems he's having rounding up the animals to go on board. He finally loses it and complains loudly to God, "You gave me a pregnant elephant but no manual for delivery!"

These questions were even incorporated into a greeting card. On the front are the words, "Profound Thought No. 566: Life is a test. It is only a test." When you open the card you read, "If this were real life, we would have been given better instructions."

I hear Jesus answering, "I have given you my principles of loving God and your neighbor. I have given you intelligence to figure out what you think is right and free will to choose it. You don't need any more. You may not be right all the time, but I trust you. All I ask is that you apply my principles as best you can. And if you live that way, doing your best to do the loving thing, then I will give you a guarantee you can count on. I promise you eternal life.

📖 The Thirty-Second Sunday of the Year
(Kg 17:10-16; Heb 9:24-28; Mk 12:38-44)

Picture the curious scene in today's gospel. Jesus was watching how much people were putting into the temple collection box. That would be like me watching what you put in our collection basket. How would you feel about that? But today's gospel is about a lot more than how much we give to the church or synagogue. When we see what is behind this gospel, giving money is going to look easy.

Back to the gospel. One poor widow came and put in two small coins worth a few cents. Then Jesus singled her out to his disciples. "Did you see that? She gave more than the others because she has contributed all she had, her whole livelihood." Have we got the scene? How do we react to this poor widow? Do we praise her for giving all she had to live on? Do we think she was downright foolish? If she didn't know where her next meal was coming from, what kind of foolishness would move her to give away the little she had? Is Jesus praising foolishness? Is Jesus asking us to be foolish?

This gospel reminds me of an incident that happened a few years ago. A man who I knew was very poor had his little girl baptized. After the baptism, and with a big smile, he gave me a $20 bill. What was I to do? I could have said, "You are being foolish. You need this more than I do." But he was so happy giving me this gift. I smiled and accepted it. Then I told him I wanted to make a gift too. I wanted him to accept this $20 to buy something nice for his little girl. He smiled and accepted it back. Of all the gifts I have received, his will always be the one I treasure most. I could never think of this man as a fool.

Is Jesus asking us to be foolish? I am not concerned here only with money. Is Jesus asking us to be foolish with our lives? There is something repugnant about the word "foolish." A father once told me about his son. He said his son can grow up to be anything he wants except a fool. But what is real foolishness? Now we touch this mystery of God's word. Do we see as God sees? What does God's word mean when it says, "Has not God turned the wisdom of this world into foolishness" (1 Cor 1)? "God chose those whom the world considers foolish to shame the wise" (1 Cor 1). What does Paul mean when he writes, "We are fools for Christ" (1 Cor 4).

I think our gospel is about a lot more than prudent use of money. I think it is about trust, letting go, and taking risks, all of which the poor widow did to the nth degree. But these words make me feel uneasy. We want to think we are in control of our lives. We want to be reasonable and prudent in all things. We plan a lot so things will turn out right. But as good as all this sounds, it does not sound very much like trust, letting go, and taking risks.

Can trust, letting go and taking risks be how God turns the wisdom of this world into foolishness? Is our worldly wisdom getting in the way of God's plan for us? Do we plan and schedule so well, and are we so logical and reasonable, that we leave little room for God, who always seems to work in us in surprising and unexpected ways? Have we felt an interior call to do something out of the ordinary and have we silenced that call with worldly wisdom which tells us it would be too risky and foolish? Have we ever been called a fool for doing something we know in our hearts was right?

In today's gospel Jesus singled out the poor widow as an example of complete trust in God. Jesus is asking us for a trust so deep that the world might call us imprudent or perhaps even foolish. When was the last time anyone called you or me a fool? I think Jesus is saying that may not be as bad as it sounds.

The Thirty-Third Sunday of the Year
(Dn 12:1-3; Heb 10:11-14, 18; Mk 13:24-32)

The last regular Sunday of our Church year always brings us a gospel about the end of the world. For some reason the end of the world fascinates us. Even though Jesus said in our gospel that no one knows when it will happen, people keep predicting the end over and over again.

Some London astrologers predicted the world would end by a flood in February, 1524. By mid-January at least 20,000 people had left their homes for higher ground. When a German scientist agreed it would happen on February 20, 1524, Count Von Iggleheim ordered a three-story ark to be built for his family. When the rain began to fall on February 20, a panicky crowd trampled the Count to death trying to board his ark. The world certainly did end for the Count.

And Jesus said, no one knows.

Many Italians had long placed their trust in the old adage, "Rome and the world are safe as long as the Coliseum stands." They got hysterical when on May 18, 1954, engineers discovered huge cracks in the Coliseum. Then someone said that doomsday would be May 24th. Thousands gathered in St. Peter's Square waiting for the end. It did not happen and builders were sent to repair the Coliseum.

And Jesus said, no one knows.

So why is Jesus talking about the end of the world? Is he trying to scare us and shock us into taking him seriously? No! Jesus does not want to scare us. How often did he say, "Do not be afraid?" I think Jesus wants us to reflect on our own lives, on the value of our limited time, and on our own end-time (our death) which is not easy.

Sure, we know death is a certainty, but we don't like to think about it. It is almost impossible for kids and young people to grasp the reality of death. It simply never enters their minds. They see themselves as eternal. That's why the death of a young person, perhaps a classmate, puts them into shock. How can this be? Death is only for old people, which to them would be anyone over thirty.

I'll never forget visiting our second grade religion class years ago. Their teacher told me they had some questions for me, and they did. Here are their questions in the exact order they asked them. "Are you married? Do you have a girlfriend? Do you have any children?" Then the little boy asked, "How old are you?" At that time I was sixty and I told him so. He just looked at me stunned and then said, "You are going to die soon." The kid made me think.

It's not easy for us grownups to think about our death. Many of you have read the book *Tuesdays with Morrie*, a book about a dying man and his former student who visits him on Tuesdays. The book is full of the wisdom that comes only from a man who knows he is dying. Morrie says, "Everybody knows they are going to die, but nobody believes it." Morrie goes on to speak to the heart of our gospel today. He speaks to the positive values of reflecting on our own end-time. "Once you learn how to die, you learn how to live. Most of us walk around as if we are sleep-walking. We don't really experience life fully. Facing death changes all that. You strip away all the stuff you are concerned with and you focus on the essentials. Then we put our priorities in order."

Wow! Wouldn't it be wonderful to come to such vision now, and to arrange our priorities and live them now?

📖 CHRIST THE KING
(Dn 7:13-19; Rv 1:5-8; Jn 18:33b-37)

Today we celebrate the feast of Christ the King.

Jesus, are you a king? "My kingdom does not belong to this world." I am not interested in titles, royal robes, or worldly power. Then you are a king, but not of this world? "For this I was born. For this I came into the world, to testify to the truth. Everyone who belongs to the truth listens to my voice."

This Feast of Christ the King is not a celebration of pomp and power. There will be no parades today, no royal floats, and no 21-gun-salutes. Today is a celebration of truth. The truth is that Jesus Christ is king. Jesus Christ is king of the universe. Jesus Christ is king of all creation. And our moment of truth is this. Is Jesus Christ your king and mine? But of course he is. Why do I even ask? Let's look at the evidence. I have his picture in my house. I have his plastic statue on my dash board. I have a crucifix around my neck. Everyone knows I am a Christian. Of course Jesus Christ is my king.

But we are not celebrating images and trappings today. Our question is still unanswered. Is Jesus Christ your king and mine? "My kingdom is not of this world. My kingdom is more powerful than this world. I ask you for more than any earthly king can ask. I want dominion over your hearts and lives, dominion is supreme authority. I simply will not and cannot settle for anything less. I am too important to you and you are too important to me to settle for second place."

How can we know if Jesus Christ is our king? Reflection on these three points can help us determine that. 1. How often do we think of Jesus? Every day? Often during the day? Do days go by without thinking of Jesus? Is Jesus only an occasional thought (more an afterthought than a predominant thought)? There can be no kingship that is an afterthought or anything less than predominant. 2. Every day we make a lot of choices, small, medium, and large choices. How much does Jesus influence our choices? Do our choices reflect care, love, and service or do they reflect caring for self, choosing self-interest over others and even at the expense of others? If Jesus plays no real part in our everyday choices, then Jesus does not have dominion over our lives. 3. When we are faced with making a moral decision where is Jesus in this decision? Does Jesus usually win or do we easily forget Jesus in favor of doing what we want, of doing what feels good, of pursuing our own gain and pleasure? When it's decision time who has dominion (supreme authority) Jesus or ourselves?

Jesus came for the truth. This is our moment of truth. In truth we all probably waffled around with these three points, "You know…yes and no…usually, but not always." But more important than how we have been is where our hearts are now. Can we say in truth, "Lord, I know the ways and the times I have not given you dominion over me. Lord, I ask your forgiveness for my failures to make you king of my life. But most importantly, I want you to be my king. I want you to take dominion over my life." If we can say this in truth, then today Jesus Christ the King can smile on us and say to you and me, "You are mine. You are not far from the kingdom."

REFLECTIONS

REFLECTIONS

REFLECTIONS